THE ANNOTATED SHAKESPEARE

Macbeth

William Shakespeare

Fully annotated, with an Introduction, by Burton Raffel

With an essay by Harold Bloom

THE ANNOTATED SHAKESPEARE

Burton Raffel, General Editor

Yale University Press · New Haven and London

"Macbeth," from *Shakespeare: The Invention of the Human,* by Harold Bloom,
copyright © 1998 by Harold Bloom. Used by permission of Riverhead Books,
an imprint of Penguin Group (USA) Inc.

Designed by Rebecca Gibb.
Set in Bembo type by The Composing Room of Michigan, Inc.
Printed in the United States of America by R. R. Donnelley & Sons.

Library of Congress Cataloging-in-Publication Data
Shakespeare, William, 1564–1616.
Macbeth / William Shakespeare ; fully annotated, with an introduction,
by Burton Raffel ; with an essay by Harold Bloom.
p.   cm. — (The annotated Shakespeare)
Includes bibliographical references.
ISBN 0-300-10654-8 (pbk.)
1. Macbeth, King of Scotland, 11th cent.—Drama.   2. Regicides—Drama.
3. Scotland—Drama.   I. Raffel, Burton.   II. Bloom, Harold.   III. Title.
PR2823.A2R34 2005
822.3'3—dc22   2004024959

A catalogue record for this book is available from the British Library.

10 9 8 7 6 5 4 3 2 1

For Evander Lomke

CONTENTS

ABOUT THIS BOOK

In act 3, scene 1, Macbeth, alone, speaks of his fears about Banquo:

> To be thus is nothing, but to be safely thus.
> Our fears in Banquo stick deep,
> And in his royalty of nature reigns that
> Which would be feared. 'Tis much he dares,
> And, to that dauntless temper of his mind,
> He hath a wisdom that doth guide his valor
> To act in safety. There is none but he
> Whose being I do fear and, under him,
> My genius is rebuked, as it is said
> Mark Antony's was by Caesar.
> (lines 48–57)

This was perfectly understandable, we must assume, to the mostly very average persons who paid to watch Elizabethan plays. But who today can make much sense of it? In this very fully annotated edition, I therefore present this passage, not in the bare form quoted above, but thoroughly supported by bottom-of-the-page notes:

To be thus[1] is nothing, but to be[2] safely thus.[3]
Our fears in[4] Banquo stick[5] deep,
And in his royalty of nature[6] reigns[7] that
Which would[8] be feared. 'Tis much he dares,
And, to[9] that dauntless temper[10] of his mind,
He hath a wisdom that doth guide his valor
To act in safety. There is none but he
Whose being[11] I do fear and, under[12] him,
My genius is rebuked,[13] as it is said
Mark Antony's was by Caesar.

The modern reader or listener may well understand many aspects of this malicious introspection. But without full explanation of words that have over the years shifted in meaning, and usages that have been altered, neither the modern reader nor the modern listener is likely to be equipped for anything like the full comprehension that Shakespeare intended and all readers or listeners deserve.

I believe annotations of this sort create the necessary bridges from Shakespeare's four-centuries-old English across to ours.

1 (i.e., the king)
2 but to be = without being
3 to be THUS is NOThing BUT to be SAFEly THUS
4 of
5 stab, thrust
6 royalty of nature = majestic character
7 predominates
8 should
9 in addition to
10 dauntless temper = bold/fearless quality of balance/calm
11 existence
12 in
13 genius is rebuked = spirit/nature is repressed/put to shame

Some readers, to be sure, will be able to comprehend unusual, historically different meanings without glosses. Those not familiar with the modern meaning of particular words will easily find clear, simple definitions in any modern dictionary. But most readers are not likely to understand Shakespeare's intended meaning, absent such glosses as I here offer.

My annotation practices have followed the same principles used in *The Annotated Milton,* published in 1999, and in my annotated editions of *Hamlet,* published (as the initial volume in this series) in 2003, and *Romeo and Juliet* (published in 2004). Classroom experience has validated these editions. Classes of mixed upper-level undergraduates and graduate students have more quickly and thoroughly transcended language barriers than ever before. This allows the teacher, or a general reader without a teacher, to move more promptly and confidently to the non–linguistic matters that have made Shakespeare and Milton great and important poets.

It is the inevitable forces of linguistic change, operant in all living tongues, which have inevitably created such wide degrees of obstacles to ready comprehension—not only sharply different meanings, but subtle, partial shifts in meaning that allow us to think we understand when, alas, we do not. Speakers of related languages like Dutch and German also experience this shifting of the linguistic ground. Like early Modern English (ca. 1600) and the Modern English now current, those languages are too close for those who know only one language, and not the other, to be readily able always to recognize what they correctly understand and what they do not. When, for example, a speaker of Dutch says, "Men kofer is kapot," a speaker of German will know that something belonging to the Dutchman is broken (*kapot* = "kaputt" in German, and *men* = "mein"). But without more linguistic awareness than the average person is apt to have, the German speaker will not identify "kofer" ("trunk" in Dutch) with "Körper"—a modern German word meaning "physique, build, body." The closest word to "kofer" in modern German, indeed, is "Scrankkoffer," which is too large a leap for ready comprehension. Speakers of different Romance languages (such as French, Spanish, or Italian), and all other related but not identical tongues, all experience these difficulties, as well as the difficulty of understanding a text written in their own language five, or six, or seven hundred years earlier. Shakespeare's English is not yet so old that it requires, like many historical texts in French and German, or like Old English texts—for example, *Beowulf*—a modern translation. Much poetry evaporates in translation: language is immensely particular. The sheer sound of Dante in thirteenth-century Italian is profoundly worth preserving. So too is the sound of Shakespeare.

I have annotated prosody (metrics) only when it seemed truly necessary or particularly helpful. Except in the few instances where modern usage syllabifies the "e," whenever an "e" in Shakespeare is *not* silent, it is marked "è". The notation used for prosody, which is also used in the explanation of Elizabethan pronunciation, follows the extremely simple form of my *From Stress to Stress: An Autobiography of English Prosody* (see "Further Reading," near the end of this book). Syllables with metrical stress are capitalized; all other syllables are in lowercase letters. I have managed to employ normalized Elizabethan spellings, in most indications of pronunciation, but I have sometimes been obliged to deviate, in the higher interest of being understood.

I have annotated, as well, a limited number of such other matters, sometimes of interpretation, sometimes of general or historical relevance, as have seemed to me seriously worthy of inclusion. These annotations have been most carefully restricted: this is not intended to be a book of literary commentary. It is for that reason that the glossing of metaphors has been severely restricted. There is almost literally no end to discussion and/or analysis of metaphor, especially in Shakespeare. To yield to temptation might well be to double or triple the size of this book—and would also change it from a historically oriented language guide to a work of an unsteadily mixed nature. In the process, I believe, neither language nor literature would be well or clearly served.

Where it seemed useful, and not obstructive of important textual matters, I have modernized spelling, including capitalization. I have frequently repunctuated. Since the original printed texts (there not being, as there never are for Shakespeare, surviving manuscripts) are frequently careless as well as self-contradictory, I have been relatively free with the wording of stage directions—and in some cases have added small directions, to indicate who is speaking to whom. I have made no emendations; I have necessarily been obliged to make choices. Textual decisions have been annotated when the differences between or among the original printed texts seem either marked or of unusual interest.

Although spelling is not on the whole a basic issue, punctuation and lineation must be given high respect. The Folio uses few exclamation marks or semicolons, which is to be sure a matter of the conventions of a very different era. Still, our modern preferences cannot be lightly substituted for what is, after a fashion, the closest thing to a Shakespeare manuscript we are likely ever to have. We do not know whether these particular seventeenth-century printers, like most of that time, were responsible for question marks, commas, periods, and, especially, all-purpose colons. But in spite of these equivocations and uncertainties, it remains true that, to a very considerable extent, punctuation tends to result from just how the mind responsible for that punctuating *hears* the text. And twenty-first-century minds have no business, in such matters, overruling seventeenth-century ones. Whoever the compositors were, they were more or less Shakespeare's contemporaries, and we are not.

Accordingly, when the original printed text uses a comma, we are being signaled that *they* (whoever "they" were) heard the text, not coming to a syntactic stop, but continuing to some later stopping point. To replace Folio commas with editorial periods is thus risky and on the whole an undesirable practice. The dramatic action of a tragedy, to be sure, may require us, for twenty-first-century readers, to highlight what four-hundred-year-old punctuation standards may not make clear—and may even, at times, misrepresent.

When the Folio text has a colon, what we are being signaled is that *they* heard a syntactic stop—though not necessarily or even usually the particular kind of syntactic stop we associate, today, with the colon. It is therefore inappropriate to substitute editorial commas for Folio colons. It is also inappropriate to employ editorial colons when *their* syntactic usage of colons does not match ours. In general, the closest thing to *their* syntactic sense of the colon is our (and their) period.

The Folio's interrogation (question) marks, too, merit extremely respectful handling. In particular, editorial exclamation marks should very rarely be substituted for the Folio's interrogation marks.

It follows from these considerations that the movement and sometimes the meaning of what we must take to be Shakespeare's *Macbeth* will at times be different, depending on whose punctuation we follow, *theirs* or our own. I have tried, here, to use the printed seventeenth-century text as a guide to both *hearing* and *understanding* what Shakespeare wrote.

In the interests of compactness and brevity, I have employed in my annotations (as consistently as I am able) a number of stylistic and typographical devices:

- The annotation of a single word does not repeat that word

- The annotation of more than one word repeats the words being annotated, which are followed by an equals sign and then by the annotation; the footnote number in the text is placed after the last of the words being annotated

- In annotations of a single word, alternate meanings are usually separated by commas; if there are distinctly different ranges of meaning, the annotations are separated by arabic numerals inside parentheses—(1), (2), and so on; in more complexly worded annotations, alternative meanings expressed by a single word are linked by a forward slash, or solidus: /

- Explanations of textual meaning are not in parentheses; comments about textual meaning are

- Except for proper nouns, the word at the beginning of all annotations is in lower case

- Uncertainties are followed by a question mark, set in parentheses: (?)

- When particularly relevant, "translations" into twenty-first-century English have been added, in parentheses

- Annotations of repeated words are not repeated. Explanations of the first instance of such common words are followed by the sign★. Readers may easily track down the first annotation, using the brief Finding List at the back of the book. Words with entirely separate meanings are annotated only for meanings no longer current in Modern English.

The most important typographical device here employed is the sign ★ placed after the first (and only) annotation of words and phrases occurring more than once. There is an alphabetically arranged listing of such words and phrases in the Finding List at the back of the book. The Finding List contains no annotations but simply gives the words or phrases themselves and the numbers of the relevant act, the scene within that act, and the foot-note number within that scene for the word's first occurrence.

Textual Note

Macbeth has only one authoritative contemporary text, the 1623 Folio. Inevitably, there are typographical (and perhaps other errors) in the Folio; these are for the most part noted, here, and sometimes discussed in the annotations to particular words and passages. We do not know whether these particular seventeenth-century typesetters tried to follow their handwritten sources. Nor do we know if those sources, or what part thereof, might have been in Shakespeare's own hand, or even whether those sources were accurate representations of what Shakespeare wrote, either in the probably first version of the play, in 1606, or in the later, revised versions that appear to have been produced. There can be (and has been) no end to speculation.

Like *Hamlet, Macbeth* is centered on its title character: Hamlet is onstage approximately 66 percent of the time, Macbeth 60 percent. Yet just as Macbeth himself is a traitor—to his king, his friends, his country, and to God—so, too, is the play steeped in both evil and betrayal. The villain of *Othello,* Iago, is arguably even more unmitigatedly evil, yet his is evil of an inexplicable, deeply individual nature. We have no idea what motivates Iago to be what he is. We see no causative connection between the world he lives in and his incredibly warped actions. He speaks, he acts, he *is* what he is; there is a total absence of rationality, a complete predominance of wildly irrational *will.* Everyone else is obliged to deal with Iago, as best they can, in terms of the inexplicably potent menace he simply is.

And yet, Macbeth is a character quite as "rational" as, say, the Satan presented to us in Milton's *Paradise Lost.* But though, like Milton's Satan, Macbeth is tormented by the evil he does, he is—also like Satan—fundamentally unable to resist. The prime importance of the witches, in this play, is in no way extrinsic: Macbeth is drawn to them, and they appear to him, because the evil aspects of his nature far outweigh the good ones. His path, from the beginning, is headed toward evil. Not only is he guided by a witches' brew, but in a very real sense he has invoked (as he soon will perform) just such profound immorality. It is apparent that evil in Macbeth's world has social and theological roots. Iago is utterly alone, but Macbeth has a great many connections, both causative and traceable, and he also has hordes of bad company.

From the first moments of the play, when the three witches take the stage—commanding it, for they have it completely to themselves—Shakespeare's audience was fully aware that the dramatic force of these three presences originated from a fiercely dangerous, socially subversive evil that everyone knew and feared. They understood perfectly the power of the demonic force engendering and supporting witches and witchcraft, which was of course Satan and his hellish underlings. And in 1606, everyone in England also knew vivid, horrific details of the deadly evil known as the Gunpowder Plot, literally meant to blow up the king and, with him, virtually every important political figure in the kingdom. Catholic dissidents were the known and indisputable instigators of this barely foiled attempt, as they were also its betrayers. (The event is commemorated on Guy Fawkes' Day, still celebrated in England every November Fifth, though now with nonlethal fireworks.)

Kings have become largely figureheads, in our time; they were still, in Shakespeare's age, the acknowledged fulcrum on which society depended and by means of whom it functioned and survived. England had been through almost a century of religious conflict, internally and externally (especially in confrontation with the major Catholic kings of Europe). Queen Elizabeth had been the target of many assassination plots; so too had James VI of Scotland, who in 1603 ascended to the English throne as James I and thus became, on the international stage, both a more visible and politically an even more important monarch.

What are now the historically more dimmed, virtually forgotten, aspects of *Macbeth*'s social and religious background require explication. But it must also be made very clear that, for a writer like Shakespeare, *theme* can and sometimes must become treatment, style, approach. Betrayal, in particular, runs like a vital bloodline through both the story and the language of *Macbeth*. It has often been noted that the movement of language, in the poetry of the play (and little of it is not in verse), is almost bewilderingly aberrant. *Macbeth*'s irregular, rough, and lurching prosody (verse movement) is not, however, the result of a text faultily transmitted but integral to the nature of a text that embodies (like Macbeth himself) deeply unnatural speech and behavior. Betrayal of earthly and heavenly kings, and of many earthly dwellers, becomes in this play a kind of infection of language itself. At times, indeed, it almost seems as if Shakespeare is so at one with his subject that he finds it hard to say virtually anything of importance in straight, unequivocal terms. Equivocation—which was then seen, in England, as the brand and trademark of evil and threatening Jesuitical language—can thus appear to us, in the early twenty-first century, every bit as bedeviling as the words of equivocators seemed to the men and women of the early seventeenth century. We are not as shocked (or as betrayed) as England then felt itself. But we can often be considerably confused.

Let me begin, as Shakespeare does in *Macbeth,* with witches and witchcraft. A witch, in Keith Thomas's useful definition, "was a person of either sex (but more often female) who could mysteriously injure other people."[1] There are two basic components, here: (1) the supernatural ("mysterious, unnatural") nature of what witches do, and (2) the doing of harm. *Maleficium,* meaning "mischief, evil," may not have been what all witches, without exception, were intending to accomplish. Yet the "white," or "good," witch can more usefully be termed a magic worker of a wholly different sort—a sorcerer or perhaps a magician. The great majority of witches clearly intended to do harm, whether they in fact succeeded or did not. A massive and widely relied upon compilation of witch lore, *Malleus Maleficarum* (The hammer of witches), published in Germany in 1486, indicates by its very title how basic an ingredient of witchery *maleficium* was considered to be. Often reprinted, the book was meant and did indeed serve as a major handbook for later witch hunters. In England, in 1689, the licensing of midwives still required an oath "that you shall not in any wise use or exercise any manner of witchcraft, charm or sorcery."[2]

Those who believed in the power of witchery of course feared it; its ability to make the supernatural world impinge on the natural one created, in their minds, immensely practical and often terrible dangers. The groundwork for witchery, in that worldview, has been vividly evoked by Thomas: "Instead of being regarded as an inanimate mass, the Earth itself was deemed to be alive. The universe was peopled by a hierarchy of spirits, and thought to manifest all kinds of occult influences and sympathies. The cosmos was an organic unity in which every part bore a sympathetic relationship to the rest. Even colours, letters and numbers were endowed with magical properties. . . . In this general intellectual climate it was easy for many magical activities to gain a plausibility which they no longer possess today."[3] The beliefs and operational procedures of religion often operate according to this same view of the world. The essential difference, plainly, is that religion does not aim at the creation of evil; rather, it aims to promote good and to combat evil.

But especially in "a witch-ridden society," such profoundly emotional matters are never clearly separable and self-contained.[4] "The early medieval Christian Church [was] alerted to the benefits of the emotional charge certain sorts of magic offered and tried hard to nourish and encourage this form of energy."[5] That is, "If the old heathen beliefs died so hard, it was precisely because they coincided at so many points with popular orthodoxy, and especially with a demonology which practically turned Christianity into a dualistic religion."[6] Extremes of poverty among the mass of people, with inevitably accompanying short and disease-racked life spans, helped create many of the elusive but pervasive bridges leading back and forth between magic and religion. Fonts of holy water, for example, had to be kept under lock and key, to keep evil practitioners from making use of the consecrated liquid's universally credited magical powers. In this and in many other ways, witches frequently exactly mirrored, in their own fashion, many of the rites and ceremonies of the Church. "The problem posed . . . by magic was one of truly gargantuan dimensions. [For the Church] it was a matter of setting aside these multifarious and vigorous competing persons [witches, etc.] . . . without dispelling the emotions and expectations which had sustained them . . . The old demons persisted into the Middle Ages . . . and occupied a prominent place . . . , partly because there was a cosmological structure and a scriptural basis ready to support them, but largely because they were a useful means of isolating persons and practices the Christian world in particular wished to proscribe—or protect."[7]

The nexus of these often violently entangled matters, for *Mac-*

beth, is the Gunpowder Plot of 1606.[8] It had been almost two years in the planning. The cellar beneath the Parliament building was packed with barrel after barrel of gunpowder. Francis Tresham, a nobleman's son, had earlier participated in the Earl of Essex's abortive rebellion (1601), and been involved in assorted other antigovernment activities conducted by recusants (Catholics who refused to attend the Church of England's Protestant services). Tresham was a leader of this new conspiracy but in the end could not accept that it would result in the death of many of his relatives. He wrote warningly to his Protestant brother-in-law, Baron Monteagle; the letter was intercepted, and the king was alerted. On November fourth, a sometime soldier and determined Catholic rebel, Guy Fawkes, was stationed underneath Parliament, waiting to light the explosives on the fifth, when the king was to open Parliament's session, with its members and many of the higher gentry and nobility in attendance. The king had ordered the basement of the building searched; Fawkes was found, arrested, and executed. Under torture, he betrayed many of the other conspirators.

Jesuits were among those most prominently implicated. The order had long been an active enemy of the Protestant church in England, as they were enemies of the monarchs who by law were at that church's head. The Jesuit priest Henry Garnett, notably, attempted to evade responsibility by "Jesuitical" equivocations, thereby heaping theological fuel on an already raging fire. Shakespeare's fellow playwright Thomas Dekker put Jesuitical equivocation in a fiercely apt nutshell: "He's brown, he's grey, he's black, he's white—/He's anything! A Jesuite! [JESuITE]."[9] A leading Protestant theologian, Lancelot Andrewes, preached bitterly: "This shrining [enshrining] it, such an abomination, setting it in the holy place, so ugly and odious, making such a treason as this a religious missal [priest's prayerbook for Mass], sacramental treason, hallowing it with orison [prayer], oath and eucharist—this passeth all the rest."[10] Sir Francis Knollys had predicted as much, in a letter dated September 29, 1581: "But the Papists' secret practices by these Jesuits, in going from house to house to withdraw men from the obedience of her Majesty [Queen Elizabeth] unto the false Catholic Church of Rome, hath and will endanger her Majesty's person and [the] state, more than all the sects of the world, if no execution shall follow upon the traitorous practicers."[11]

King James had a longstanding and profound, even professional, interest in witches and witchery. In 1597, while still King of Scotland, he had composed an earnest treatise on the subject, *Daemonologie*. His government launched a long, extensive campaign to brand the Gunpowder Plot and the Jesuits as witchlike evil. Both these negatives and a strongly, even a glowing, portrayal of King James were "spread energetically through all the media."[12] In 1608 the Protestant divine, William Perkins, preached a sermon that nicely expresses one of the major thrusts of this campaign. "It were a thousand times better for the land, if all witches . . . might suffer death."[13]

And so to the play that Shakespeare wrote. Perhaps the most effective way of indicating at least some of the complexity and taut dramatic structure of *Macbeth* is an analysis of the seven scenes of act 1. ("In my end," ran Mary Queen of Scots's motto, "is my beginning.") "I'll do, I'll do, and I'll do," intones Witch 1 (1.3.9), and her extremely simple words vibrate with fearful, unspoken evil. The effect is all the greater because, in scene 2, the rhetorical pitch has been flagrantly elevated—ratcheted up so remarkably high, indeed, that many commentators have convinced themselves Shakespeare could not have written such stuff. Yet this second scene itself is similarly, and most carefully, made contrastive to scene 1, in which the witches begin the play with equally plain-seeming words, once again fraught with unexpressed and perhaps inexpressible significance: "When shall we three meet again/In thunder, lightning, or in rain?" (1.1.1–2). The sergeant's language in scene 2 splashes like dramatic pastels, immensely colorful. But its true significance is the portrayal of (a) the gaping, credulous king, and (b) the high, bright light in which the figure of Macbeth, not yet onstage, is presented. "O valiant cousin, worthy gentleman!" exclaims Duncan (1.2.24). The exalted bravery of "our captains, Macbeth and Banquo" (1.2.34), soars rhetorically to almost fairy-tale heights, complete with references to sparrows, eagles, hares, and lions, the animal figures of fable and legend. The badly wounded sergeant finally goes off, but immediately Ross comes on, looking as one "should . . . look / That seems to speak things strange" (1.2.46–47). Ross's account of battling the King of Norway maintains both Macbeth's glorious military standing and the scene's lofty rhetoric at high levels.

Let us step back, for a moment, to the intentionally very different language of scene 1 and the first portion of scene 3. How recreate, for a modern audience, what was for the men and women of Shakespeare's time the tremulously awful juxtaposition of (1) witches and (2) the natural signs and symbols of their ghastly power? Shakespeare's audience not only had a greater sense for spoken stylistic tonalities,[14] but it also had an immediate appreciation, for example, for the magical significance of the number three—"we three," and the thrice-iterated "I'll do." They responded very differently to night ("'ere the set of sun"), as well as to darkness in daytime ("fog and filthy air"). Night was a thoroughly and notoriously unreliable, savagely dangerous period, full of active and overwhelmingly evil spirits of all kinds (it was for good reason known as the "witching" time), and darkness in daytime was precisely the kind of unnatural inversion these witches proclaim in the final line of scene 1, "Fair is foul, and foul is fair" (1.1.12). There was nothing casual, nor anything merely pictorial about such inversions. Shakespeare's audience *could* not take the unnatural lightly, nor could they afford to treat witchery with indifference. Witches dancing their magic circles, with or without music, were not matters of entertainment, or of fun. When the three witches exclaim, "the charm's wound up" ("ready"), Shakespeare's audience knew in their very bones that horrible things were in store. Charms—more like modern explosives than anything decorative—were the very farthest thing from "charming."

And when in the second portion of scene 3 Macbeth finally appears on stage, together with Banquo, he first speaks only a brief line: "So foul and fair a day I have not seen" (1.3.39). Early seventeenth-century ears immediately recognized the echoing of earlier witch words and knew exactly what that replication indicated. To this point, the audience has only heard *about* Macbeth, but the witches have just announced his coming (saying nothing of Banquo)—and their powers of prediction are, as they are meant to be, uncanny ("uncomfortably unnatural"). It is left to Banquo to register onstage awareness of the witches' presence, and to comment about their "withered and wild" appearance. Banquo's response to the very sight of witches surely comes very close to what the audience's response would have been. Banquo clearly dwells in the seventeenth century's world of normal realities. But does Macbeth dwell there too? The witches do not answer Banquo's string of queries, nor is there is any accident about their silence. Macbeth and Macbeth alone is the focus of their attentions. And the attention of witches was, for men and women of that time, at best a dubious blessing. But for Macbeth?

Again, he speaks sparsely: "Speak, if you can. What are you?" (1.3.49). Macbeth actively and directly desires their speech; this is yet another clear warning of evils to come. "What manner of person are you? Who are you?" he has asked. And evil then advances to meet him, as the witches do indeed address him, in extravagantly prophetic, and cloaked, slippery, only apparently complimentary terms. Macbeth's advancements in status, of which he has had as yet no knowledge, are proclaimed, in the witches' typically plain-seeming but deceptive language. And Banquo, watching his military colleague, informs us that Macbeth is surprised, as he should be, and upset, as he should not be. Are not such great leaps in status exactly what he wants? Macbeth does not respond to Banquo's questions.

Banquo then asks the witches for information about himself, and in apparently much the same manner is given it. He is "lesser" than Macbeth, but "greater"; he is not as "happy," "yet much happier" (1.3.65, 66). But the apparent similarity in the witches' responses, as between the two men, thinly cloaks major unlikenesses. Macbeth will rise to grand heights. Period. But in a fashion far less direct, Banquo will rise to "get kings, though thou be none" (1.3.68). Lineage was a profoundly serious matter in Shakespeare's time. Fathers understood that they lived on, after death, primarily in their children, most particularly their sons. A profoundly Christian culture, accepting that the human soul survived physical death, understandably stressed this physical survival as well. Banquo's rewards do not, on the surface, seem so large as Macbeth's, but the audience knew they were in fact considerably greater. Significantly, Banquo is not at all sure these creatures can or should be trusted. He understands, in other words, that all things come to us with price tags attached—and, when witches are selling, let the buyer beware.

There is betrayal on all sides, here, to right and to left. There is verbal sliding about, and though we may not yet realize its exact extent or its character, Shakespeare's audience had heard enough to smell a rat, and to pretty specifically identify the filthy beast. Equivocation was emphatically blowing in the wind. And Macbeth's response? He speaks nine full lines, full of intensely self-absorbed demands, ending, "Speak, I charge you" (1.3.79). We learn in due course that he too is lying, as he so regularly does. His claim that "To be king / Stands not within the prospect of belief" (1.3.74–75) runs directly in the face of the disclosure, later in the play, that he has already been plotting the death of the king and his own ascension, as a close relative in the same royal lineage, to the throne. Why does he bother lying to the witches? (But why does Satan, in *Paradise Lost,* lie to his fellow fallen angels?) And does Macbeth seriously expect the witches to explain "from whence / [they] owe this strange intelligence" (1.3.76–77)? He can have no doubt—Shakespeare's audience surely did not—why the witches had appeared, and had spoken "such prophetic greeting," to him (1.3.79). Witches are in only one distinctly limited line of business, which is the doing of evil. Macbeth has no apparent awareness—or concern?—about matters that everyone then knew. Why? Which side of the eternal struggle between good and evil, between God and Satan, is Macbeth on? Shakespeare's audience could have had no doubt, by now, about this, either.

Ross arrives; the witches seem to have spoken truthfully—and Macbeth, in a series of musing "asides" (by seventeenth-century dramatic convention, not heard by anyone onstage not meant by the speaker to hear), gives still further evidence of deceit and treachery. "Glamis, and Thane of Cawdor. / The greatest is behind" (1.3.116–117). The implication is starkly plain: Macbeth intends, and has intended, to do still more by way of advancing himself. Less plain, perhaps, is the fact that what must come next is the murder of the king. This is wonderfully highlighted by having Macbeth first thank Ross for the welcome news and then immediately turn to Banquo and discuss ascendance to the throne: "Do you not hope your children shall be kings, / When those that gave the Thane of Cawdor to me / Promised no less to them?" (1.3.118–120).

Banquo raises an honest man's doubts about dealing with "the instruments of darkness," then turns to converse with Ross and Angus. Macbeth, delighted at the witches' now proven accuracy, is even more delighted at his own prospects. "Two truths are told, / As happy prologues to the swelling act / of the imperial theme" (1.3.127–129). The "swelling act" can only be, for him—and who knew this better than Shakespeare's audience?—Duncan's murder. The equivocator's language remains equally plain, even when Macbeth speaks to himself.

Either Banquo's admonition or Macbeth's own awareness of the supernatural leads Macbeth to ponder, "This supernatural soliciting / Cannot be ill, cannot be good" (1.3.130–131). The inversion of priorities is subtle but significant: first comes the judgment that it cannot be evil, and only then, weakly, does Macbeth acknowledge (or merely say?) that it cannot be good. His self-deception is typical of a man well along on the road to hell (in

which awful destination at least 99.9 percent of Shakespeare's audience devoutly and tremblingly believed). His self-centeredness
is appalling: how can this be evil, when it tells *me* the good things
I want to hear? But if this is all truly good, why, he asks himself, in
language fantastic and opaque, "do I yield to that suggestion /
Whose horrid image doth unfix my hair / And make my seated
heart knock at my ribs, / Against the use of nature?" (1.3.134–
137). His temptation ("suggestion"), as we have already seen, does
not stem from the witches' words. The "horrid image" is one he
has contemplated before and has not abandoned. Indeed, "Present
fears," he goes on, "Are less than horrible imaginings" (1.3.137–
138). That is, a deed in hand, in process, is nowhere near so awful
as we have thought, in only imagining it. Self-betrayal can virtually be seen crossing over into the betrayal, and the murder, of his
king. And Macbeth's next words provide all the confirmation
one might want: "My thought, whose murder yet is but fantastical" (1.3.139). So too his equivocating is terribly apparent to us,
though not to him: "nothing is / but what is not" (1.3.141–142).

Macbeth is quite obviously (as Banquo observes) "rapt." Banquo, good man that he is, explains how strange and wonderful, as
yet, Macbeth's "new honors" are to him. He will adjust to them,
given time. But Macbeth is not so much rapt (in a state of "rap-
ture") as rolling in the mud and muck of self-indulgent conjec-
ture and longing. "If chance will have me king, why, chance may
crown me" (1.3.143). It is not that he is deeply loath to kill Duncan; rather, he would very much prefer to have the crown handed
to him. He finishes the thought with "chance may crown me, /
Without my stir" (1.3.143–144). And wouldn't that be nice? Let
lightning and thunder, or a falling tree, do my work. Equivocation cannot be more plain, or less genuinely communicative, than

"Time and the hour runs through the roughest day" (1.3.147). That is, no matter what man may do ("Come what come may," 1.3.146), the present will become the past.

We can thus see why, as scene 4 opens, Malcolm tells the pungent tale of the prior Thane of Cawdor's graveside repentance. "Nothing in his life / Became him like the leaving it" (1.4.7–8). Unlike the high rhetoric of scene 2, this is as plain as plain can be, as well as far more moral than witch-style plainness: Cawdor died far, far better than he lived. This comports with Malcolm's father's, the king's, wonderfully outgoing words to Macbeth and is starkly contrasted with Macbeth's completely deceitful response, which not only professes humble and devoted loyalty to Duncan but vows to do "everything / Safe toward [protective of] your love and honor" (1.4.26–27). When therefore Duncan declares his intention of at once visiting Macbeth's home, to confer upon the new Thane of Cawdor "signs of nobleness . . . And bind us [me] further to you" (1.4.41–43), Macbeth's reply cannot help but be chilling to an audience that has just a moment before been privy to the new Thane of Cawdor's murderous mind. Can Macbeth possibly mean to be the simple messenger of good news, in hurrying back to his wife? No: that is the answer we hear at once from Macbeth himself. Macbeth has just heard, from the king's mouth, that Malcolm is now the proclaimed heir to the throne. The news should not be dreadfully surprising to someone as "humble" as Macbeth pretends to be, but to Macbeth it is devastating. If a tree falls on Duncan's head, after this, his successor is already arranged. It will be Duncan's elder son, Malcolm. It will not be Macbeth. "I must fall down, or else o'er leap," he declares in an aside, "For in my way it lies." And then he calls for darkness, not light, to prevail. "Let . . . The eye wink at the hand." To which invocation he adds, at once: "Yet let that be / Which the eye fears, when it is done, to see" (1.4.49–50, 51–52, 52–53). "Fantastical" thoughts of murder will no longer linger, inactive, in his mind. Duncan's time has come— and Malcolm's will follow, one way or another.

To this point, we know absolutely nothing of Lady Macbeth. The process of informing us begins with a rush, with a swift transition to the lady, coming onto an otherwise empty stage, reading aloud a letter sent her by her husband. When his letter declares her to be his "dearest partner of greatness" (1.5.10), the audience is promptly shown that she is instigative (bad), not at all the passive creature a conventional wife (good) was expected to be. Not surprisingly, she does not know all there is to know about the secrets of her husband's heart. She worries that Macbeth is insufficiently determined and that he is "too full o' the milk of human kindness" (1.5.15). Men did not think a great deal of "milk"; women did. But just as her husband turns morality on its head, so too does his wife. Who but another equivocator could turn that which is uniquely life-sustaining into that which, in the name of ambition, is murderous? She is manifestly self-deceived, as both husband and wife frequently are, when she says that Macbeth "would not [does not wish/want to] play false" (1.5.19). He too is only deceiving himself, on this score. Shakespeare's audience already knew better, and we should, as well. But Duncan's imminent death is certain—so certain, Lady Macbeth, declares, that "the raven . . . is hoarse, / That croaks the fatal entrance of Duncan / Under my battlements" (1.5.36–38). Not "our" battlements, or "these" battlements, but "my" battlements: she is indeed a full partner in the Macbeth enterprise.

And how like her husband's, though much more single-minded, is her declaration of "direst cruelty," of "my fell purpose"

(1.5.41, 44). He will do what needs to be done; he has said so, and will, as we will learn, act accordingly. She has, at least for the moment, a clearer recognition of the necessary deed.

Macbeth's stumbling reply to her question about when the king "goes hence" is reluctant rather than truly hesitant: "Tomorrow, as he purposes" (1.5.58). Had he said simply "tomorrow," it would not have been an equivocating answer; a simple declarative statement this most surely is not. Duncan "intends" to leave tomorrow. "Never," responds Lady Macbeth. "We will speak further," equivocates Macbeth. No, she assures him. Just "leave all the rest to me" (1.5.69−71).

Set against scene 5, in which the unwomanly (and therefore "unnatural") attitudes of Lady Macbeth would have seemed infinitely more shocking to Shakespeare's audience than they are likely to be today, scene 6 begins in a deliberately bucolic, pastoral mode. Well-intentioned but rather simple-minded Duncan, who has informed us in scene 4 that Macbeth's predecessor as Thane of Cawdor "was a gentleman on whom I built / An absolute trust" (1.4.13−14), opens scene 6 by happily declaiming, "This castle hath a pleasant seat. The air / Nimbly and sweetly recommends itself" (1.6.1−2). Banquo courteously and good-heartedly joins him. Duncan greets Lady Macbeth's entrance with similarly misguided praise. And Lady Macbeth, predictably, puts on a facile show of humble welcome. But the echo of her "Come, thick night, / And pall thee in the dunnest smoke of hell" (1.5.48−49) is still resounding in our ears. Duncan may take her hand and graciously join her in entering the castle. But no audience whatever can be similarly taken in.

Other than scene 3 and its fuller presentation of the witches, containing as well as a substantial introduction to Macbeth and

Banquo, scene 7 is the longest of the first act. With the swift, jarring juxtapositions typical of the entire play, it opens with Macbeth, standing alone outside the dining hall, obviously not so much hesitant about murder as, by nature, inclined to fence sitting. "If it were done, when 'tis done, then 'twere well / It were done quickly" (1.7.1–2). As before, what seems uncertainty or hesitation in Macbeth is merely equivocal self-deception: "*If* it were done" may perhaps seem to be entirely suppositional. But "if" is also a markedly weasel-like word, having in it plain and well-established shades of "granted that," "if not, why not," and almost but not quite reaching "when." Macbeth proceeds to discuss "assassination" and its consequences, making it plain that he fears the consequences, and not the assassination itself. He starts to probe himself in religious terms—"But in these cases / We still [always] have [receive] judgment here" (1.7.7–8)—which, after a brief consideration of loyalty and trust, he turns into what reveals itself as a concern for public relations. "[Duncan's] virtues / will plead like angels, trumpet tongued, against / The deep damnation of his taking off" (1.7.18–20). He worries about the effect of "pity" for the murdered king, and the drastic blowing of "the horrid deed in every eye." (1.7.21, 24).

Macbeth is interrupted by his wife, demanding to know, "Why have you left the chamber?" He naturally equivocates: "Hath he asked for me?" (1.7.30–31). This is rather a dull-witted avoidance gesture, hardly well calculated to put off a charging tigress. The lady's response is bitingly ironic: "Know you not he has?" Macbeth straightens his back, significantly choosing to declare that "We will proceed no further in this business"—but not on moral grounds, or even for fear of other consequences. It is public relations on which he tries to take his stand: "I have bought / Golden opinions from all sorts of people, / Which would [ought to] be worn now in their newest gloss, / Not cast aside so soon" (1.7.33−36). As we will discover once he has become king, Macbeth is not a man much beholden to public opinion. It is hard to think of him, even in this first act, as even vaguely resembling an honest man. We have seen and heard too much meanness and lying. If we assume, however, that he is truly purposeful about not wanting to proceed with the murder, we may ask ourselves why he proceeds to hand her the very key to his nature, asserting that "I dare do all that may become a man." Without any hesitation whatever, she pounces on this weaseling excuse. I'd have killed the baby I was suckling, she proclaims, "had I so sworn / As you have done to this" (1.7.47−60). All he can do is whine; the battle between them, if it has ever been that, is as good as done. "If we should fail?" She soars: "What cannot you and I perform . . . ?" (1.7.60, 70).

He is remarkably cheerful about giving in—if that is indeed what he does. "Bring forth men children only" (1.7.73), he assures her, and then delightedly chortles about how well the whole thing will surely work. She agrees, and he ends the act by affirming, "I am settled," accepting without further protest the remainder of the banquet's inevitable burdens of active duplicity. He agrees to "mock the time with fairest show," since "False face must hide what the false heart doth know" (1.7.80−83). They go back to the banquet together, manifestly blithe and resolved. Macbeth does, later in the play, like to think of himself as a victim, when things start to go wrong. But at the close of act 1 he has been heading in murderous directions for too long, suddenly to turn and throw over the conspiracy. It has not been a close call, this husband-and-wife discussion. Can we believe that he really wanted to "prevail," by getting out of the assassination? He wants, rather, to become king. That is not only what he does, it is in the nature of things the only thing he can do, the only thing he can accept.

Notes

1. Keith Thomas, *Religion and the Decline of Magic: Studies in Popular Beliefs in Sixteenth and Seventeenth Century England* (New York: Oxford University Press, 1997), 436.
2. David Cressy, *Birth, Marriage and Death: Ritual, Religion, and the Life-Cycle in Tudor and Stuart England* (Oxford: Oxford University Press, 1997), 65.
3. Thomas, *Religion and the Decline of Magic,* 223.
4. Theodore K. Rabb, *The Struggle for Stability in Early Modern Europe* (New York: Oxford University Press, 1975), 116.
5. Valerie I. J. Flint, *The Rise of Magic in Early Medieval Europe* (Princeton, N.J.: Princeton University Press, 1991), 4.
6. G. G. Coulton, *Five Centuries of Religion,* 4 vols. (Cambridge: Cambridge University Press, 1923), 1:66.
7. Flint, *Rise of Magic,* 71, 107.
8. The story is powerfully retold, and the linkages detailed, in Gary Wills, *Witches and Jesuits: Shakespeare's "Macbeth"* (New York: Oxford University Press, 1995), 13–31.
9. Wills, *Witches and Jesuits,* 97.
10. Florence Higham, *Lancelot Andrewes* (London: SCM Press, 1952), 46.
11. Alexander J. Ellis, *On Early English Pronunciation, with Especial Reference to Shakspere and Chaucer,* pt. 1 (London: Trübner, 1867), 36.
12. Wills, *Witches and Jesuits,* 31.
13. John Chandos, ed., *In God's Name: Examples of Preaching in England, 1534–1662* (Indianapolis, Ind.: Bobbs-Merrill, 1971), 135.
14. See Burton Raffel, "Metrical Dramaturgy in Shakespeare's Earlier Plays," *CEA Critic* 57, no. 3 (1995): 51–65, and Raffel, "Who Heard the Rhymes, and How: Shakespeare's Dramaturgical Signals," *Oral Tradition* 11, no. 2 (1996): 190–221.

SOME ESSENTIALS OF
THE SHAKESPEAREAN STAGE

The Stage

- There was no *scenery* (backdrops, flats, and so on).

- There were virtually no *on-stage props,* only an occasional chair or table, a cup or flask.

- *Costumes* (which belonged to and were provided by the individual actors) were very elaborate. As in most premodern and very hierarchical societies, clothing was the distinctive mark of who and what a person was.

- What the actors *spoke,* accordingly, contained both the dramatic and narrative material we have come to expect in a theater (or movie house) and (a) the setting, including details of the time of day, the weather, and so on, and (b) the occasion. The *dramaturgy* is thus very different from that of our own time, requiring much more attention to verbal and gestural matters. Strict realism was neither intended nor, under the circumstances, possible.

- There was *no curtain.* Actors entered and left via the side of the stage.

- In *public* theaters, there was no *lighting;* performances could take place only in daylight hours.

- For *private* theaters, located in large halls of aristocratic houses, candlelight illumination was possible.

The Actors

- Actors worked in *professional* for-profit companies, sometimes organized and owned by other actors, and sometimes by entrepreneurs who could afford to erect or rent the company's building. Public theaters could hold, on average, a probable two-thousand-size audience, most of whom viewed and listened while standing. Significant profits could be and were made. Private theaters were smaller, more exclusive; profit-making was not an issue.

- There was *no stage director.* A prompter, presumably standing in one wing, had a text marked with entrances and exits; a few of these survive. Rehearsals seem to have been largely group affairs; we know next to nothing of the dynamics involved or from what sort of texts individual actors worked. However, we do know that, probably because Shakespeare's England was largely an oral culture, actors learned their parts rapidly and retained them intact for years. This was *repertory* theater, regularly repeating popular plays and introducing some new ones each year.

- *Women* were not permitted on the professional stage. All female parts were acted by prepubescent *boys.*

The Audience

- London's professional theater operated in what might be called a "red-light" district, featuring brothels, restaurants, and the kind of *open-air entertainment* then most popular, like bear-baiting (in which a bear, tied to a stake, was set on by dogs).

- A theater audience, like most of the population of Shakespeare's England, was largely made up of *illiterates.* Being able to read and write, however, had nothing to do with intelligence or concern with language, narrative, and characterization. People attracted to the theater tended to be both extremely verbal and extremely volatile. Actors were sometimes attacked, when the audience was dissatisfied; quarrels and fights were relatively common. Women were commonly in attendance, though no reliable statistics exist.

- Plays were almost never *printed,* during Shakespeare's lifetime. Not only did drama not have the cultural esteem it has in our time, but neither did literature in general. Shakespeare wrote a good deal of nondramatic poetry yet so far as we know did not authorize or supervise whatever of his work appeared in print during his lifetime.

- Playgoers, who had paid good money to see and hear, plainly gave dramatic performances very careful, detailed attention. For some closer examination of such matters, see Burton Raffel, "Who Heard the Rhymes and How: Shakespeare's Dramaturgical Signals," *Oral Tradition* 11 (October 1996): 190–221, and Raffel, "Metrical Dramaturgy in Shakespeare's Earlier Plays," *CEA Critic* 57 (Spring–Summer 1995): 51–65.

Macbeth

CHARACTERS (DRAMATIS PERSONAE)

Duncan (king of Scotland)

Malcolm (the king's older son and heir)

Donalbain (the king's younger son)

Macbeth (Scottish nobleman and a general of the king's army)

Banquo (Scottish nobleman and a general of the king's army)

Fleance (Banquo's son)

Macduff (Scottish nobleman)

Boy (Macduff's son)

Lennox (Scottish nobleman)

Ross (Scottish nobleman)

Menteith (Scottish nobleman)

Angus (Scottish nobleman)

Caithness (Scottish nobleman)

Siward (Earl of Northumberland and English general)

Young Siward (his son)

Seyton (servant to Macbeth)

Doctor (English)

Doctor (Scottish)

Soldier

Porter

Old Man

Murderers

Lady Macbeth

Lady Macduff

Gentlewoman (servant to Lady Macbeth)

Hecat (Hecate)

Witches

Apparitions

Lords, Soldiers, Servants, Messengers

Act I

An open place, near Forres[1]

LIGHTNING AND THUNDER. ENTER THREE WITCHES

Witch 1 When shall we three meet again
  In thunder, lightning, or in rain?[2]
Witch 2 When the hurlyburly's[3] done,
  When the battle's lost and won.
Witch 3 That will be ere[4] the set of sun.[5]   5
Witch 1 Where the place?
Witch 2   Upon the heath.[6]

---

1 site of Duncan's royal palace (about 25 mi NNE of Inverness)
2 WHEN shall WE three MEET aGAIN / in THUNder LIGHTning OR in RAIN (note that neither punctuation nor syntax are incorporated in scansions, since poetic meter does not depend on either)
3 turmoil, fighting, rebellion – the last being the occasion of the "battle" mentioned in the next line: witches thronged to battlefields, needing human body parts for their black magic ("hurlyburly" has become an essentially jocular word but in Shakespeare's time was deadly serious)
4 before★
5 that WILL be ERE the SET of SUN
6 bare, open land, uncultivated, flat, and often wild★

Witch 3 There to meet with Macbeth.

Witch 1 I come, Graymalkin!⁷

Witch 2 Paddock⁸ calls.

Witch 3   Anon!⁹

10   *All*   Fair is foul, and foul is fair.¹⁰

        Hover¹¹ through the fog¹² and filthy¹³ air.

EXEUNT¹⁴

7 then-common name for a cat: Witch 1 has heard and is responding to the call
   of her familiar spirit, a demon associated with and in a witch's power
   (grayMALkin)
8 frog, toad: again, this is Witch 2's familiar spirit
9 at once*
10 (that which is fine/beautiful* is [to witches as to other evil spirits] ugly/
   disgusting/dirty, and that which is ugly/disgusting/dirty is [to them] fine/
   beautiful, since they live, and glory, in the upside-down, inside-out world of
   the devil)
11 hang in the air, witches having the (nocturnal) power of flight: see note 12,
   below
12 dense, dark vapor (Vapors, or exhalations, were considered noxious, causing
   disease and death, and were often associated with evil creatures and their
   deeds; witches' powers of flight were fully operative in the dark, but
   diminished or blocked by ordinary daylight, which was unmistakably
   overwhelmed, on this particular day, by "fog and filthy air." This is esoteric
   knowledge, in our time, but was universally understood by Shakespeare and
   his audience – the latter, certainly, overwhelmingly serious about witches'
   capacity for evil)
13 dirty *and* defiled ("filthy" air or water is murky, thick, and often turbulent)
14 exeunt = "they exit"

SCENE 2
A battlefield camp, near Forres[1]

ALARUM[2] WITHIN.[3] ENTER DUNCAN, MALCOLM, DONALBAIN,
LENNOX, WITH SERVANTS AND A BLEEDING SERGEANT

Duncan   What bloody[4] man is that? He can report,
As seemeth by his plight,[5] of the revolt[6]
The newest state.[7]

Malcolm   This is the sergeant[8]
Who like a good and hardy[9] soldier fought
'Gainst my captivity.[10] Hail, brave friend.[11]   5
Say to the king the knowledge of the broil[12]
As thou didst leave it.

Sergeant   Doubtful it stood,
As two spent[13] swimmers, that do cling together
And choke their art.[14] The merciless Macdonwald –

1 FORres
2 call to arms, usually sounded by a trumpet
3 inside (i.e., offstage)★
4 covered with blood (not recorded as an epithet until the late 18th c.)
5 as seemeth by his plight = it appears from/because of his dangerous condition
6 (the rebellion is directed against Duncan, King of Scotland)
7 state of affairs (the newest state of the revolt)
8 ambiguous classification, meaning middle-ranking officer, common soldier,
   or servant: the 1623 Folio text, in this scene, describes him as a "Captaine," a
   "Serieant" (sergeant), and also as "a good and hardie Souldier"
9 courageous, bold
10 probably an attempt to take him prisoner
11 not as clear a word as it has become, today: Malcolm probably uses it as a sign
   of princely goodwill and gratitude, rather than as a declaration of friendship
12 tumult, fight
13 exhausted
14 choke their art = block/interfere with each other's skillful actions: the
   primary meaning of "art"★ was the application of acquired skills or of
   learning

10   Worthy to be a rebel, for to that[15]
     The multiplying villainies of nature
     Do swarm[16] upon him – from the western isles[17]
     Of[18] kerns[19] and gallowglasses[20] is supplied,
     And Fortune, on his damnèd quarrel[21] smiling,
15   Showed like[22] a rebel's whore.[23] But all's too weak,[24]
     For brave Macbeth – well he deserves that name –
     Disdaining Fortune, with his brandished[25] steel,
     Which smoked with bloody execution,[26]
     Like valor's minion[27] carvèd out his passage[28]
20   Till he faced the slave[29] –
     Which[30] ne'er shook hands, nor bade farewell to him,
     Till he unseamed[31] him from the nave[32] to th' chops,[33]
     And fixed[34] his head upon our battlements.[35]

15 for to that = because
16 gather in a cluster
17 the western isles = the Hebrides
18 with
19 lightly armed Irish foot soldiers★
20 axe-wielding horsemen
21 cause
22 showed like = appeared to be
23 (i.e., "satisfying"/favoring the rebels: Fortune is a goddess)
24 all's too weak = it (Fortune)/they (the rebels) was/were too wavering,
   lacking courage/strength of purpose
25 flourished, displayed
26 action, accomplishment – and, by extension, "slaughter" (EXeCUsiON)
27 beloved favorite/darling
28 movement, way
29 rascal★ (Macdonwald)
30 who (i.e., Macbeth: Renaissance syntax often does *not* follow the rules of
   21st-c. English)
31 ripped up
32 navel
33 jaws
34 placed, fastened
35 protective covering on top of fortified walls★

Duncan   O valiant[36] cousin,[37] worthy gentleman![38]

Sergeant As whence[39] the sun 'gins his reflection,[40]   25

    Shipwrecking storms and direful thunders break,

    So from that spring[41] whence comfort seemed to come

    Discomfort swells.[42] Mark,[43] King of Scotland, mark:

    No sooner justice[44] had, with valor armed,[45]

    Compelled these skipping[46] kerns to trust[47] their heels,   30

    But the Norweyan lord,[48] surveying vantage,[49]

    With furbished[50] arms and new supplies of men

    Began a fresh assault.

Duncan   Dismayed not this

    Our captains,[51] Macbeth and Banquo?

Sergeant   Yes —

    As sparrows eagles,[52] or the hare the lion.   35

    If I say sooth,[53] I must report they were

36 courageous, strong
37 loosely used to describe a variety of blood relatives, close and not so close★ (Duncan and Macbeth share a grandfather)
38 worthy gentleman = excellent★ man of high birth★
39 as whence = just as occurs/is caused when (i.e., the syntactical movement runs: "Just as the sun beginning to shine [which is good] causes storms (which are bad), so too what had appeared to be a source of comfort [to the rebels] became a source of grief")
40 action, shining (reFLEKseeOWN)
41 source of flowing water (i.e., Macdonwald, leader of the rebellion)
42 increases, grows, rises
43 notice★
44 moral righteousness
45 (adjective modifying "valor")
46 hopping, running
47 place their reliance on
48 Norwegian king (a rebel ally)
49 surveying vantage = observing an advantage/profitable opportunity
50 polished, brightened
51 generals (as in the 19th-c. phrase "captains of industry")
52 as sparrows eagles = as sparrows dismay eagles (i.e., not at all)
53 truth★

As cannons overcharged[54] with double cracks,[55]

So they[56] doubly redoubled strokes upon the foe.[57]

Except[58] they meant to bathe in reeking[59] wounds,

40 Or memorize[60] another Golgotha,[61]

I cannot tell.

But I am faint, my gashes[62] cry for help.

Duncan So well thy words become[63] thee as thy wounds,

They smack[64] of honor both. Go get him surgeons.[65]

EXIT SERGEANT, ATTENDED

ENTER ROSS, WITH ANGUS

Who comes here?[66]

45 *Malcolm*   The worthy Thane[67] of Ross.

Lennox What a haste looks through[68] his eyes. So should he[69] look

That seems to speak things strange.

Ross   God save the king!

Duncan Whence cam'st thou, worthy Thane?

54 overloaded
55 roars (i.e., that which makes a cannon roar: gunpowder)
56 Macbeth and Banquo
57 SO they DOUbly reDOUBled STROKES upON the FOE
58 whether
59 steaming (freshly made)
60 memorialize, perpetuate the memory of
61 burial place, charnel house
62 wounds★
63 suit, agree with★
64 savor
65 doctors/medical men generally
66 WHO comes HERE
67 baron, clan chief (in Scotland, equivalent to an earl's son)
68 looks through = looks from/out of (what a HASTE looks THROUGH)
69 someone

Ross   From Fife,[70]

    great king,
    Where the Norweyan banners flout[71] the sky
    And fan[72] our people cold.   50
    Norway himself, with terrible numbers,[73]
    Assisted by that most disloyal traitor,[74]
    The Thane of Cawdor, began a dismal[75] conflict,
    Till that[76] Bellona's bridegroom,[77] lapped in proof,[78]
    Confronted him with self comparisons,[79]   55
    Point against point, rebellious arm 'gainst arm,[80]
    Curbing[81] his lavish[82] spirit – and, to conclude,
    The victory fell on us.

Duncan   Great happiness!

Ross   That[83] now
    Sweno, the Norways' king, craves composition,[84]
    Nor would we deign[85] him burial of his men   60

---

70 roughly 25 mi. N of Edinburgh
71 mock (because there are so many of them)
72 blow, drive
73 terrible numbers = a very great number of men
74 asSISTed BY that MOST disLOYal TRAITor
75 unlucky, disastrous
76 till that = until
77 Bellona's bridegroom = Macbeth (Bellona = warlike wife of the god of war, Mars)
78 lapped in proof = wrapped/clothed in impenetrable, well-tested armor (till THAT belLONa's BRIDEgroom LAPPed in PROOF)
79 self comparisons = equivalents to his own power
80 rebellious arm 'gainst arm = rebel arms against loyal arms
81 restraining, checking
82 impetuous, wild
83 so that
84 the settling of differences
85 condescend to give/grant

Till he disbursèd,[86] at Saint Colme's Inch,[87]

Ten thousand dollars[88] to our general[89] use.

Duncan   No more that Thane of Cawdor shall deceive[90]

Our bosom[91] interest. Go pronounce his present[92] death,

65   And with his former title greet Macbeth.

Ross   I'll see it done.

Duncan   What he hath lost, noble Macbeth hath won.

EXEUNT

86 paid
87 Saint Colme's Inch = small island in the Firth of Forth, off Edinburgh
   (COLme's)
88 (a sum impossible to explain: Shakespeare here uses "dollars," but the Spanish
   coins of that name were not minted until half a millennium after these words
   were supposedly spoken)
89 communal, national
90 betray
91 dearest
92 immediate, instant★

SCENE 3
A heath

THUNDER. ENTER THE THREE WITCHES

Witch 1 Where hast thou been, sister?

Witch 2 Killing swine.[1]

Witch 3 Sister, where thou?[2]

Witch 1 A sailor's wife had chestnuts in her lap,

And munched, and munched, and munched.[3]   5

"Give me," quoth[4] I.

"Aroint[5] thee, witch!" the rump-fed ronyon[6] cries.

Her husband's to Aleppo[7] gone, master[8] o' the *Tiger*,

But in a sieve[9] I'll thither sail,

And, like a rat without a tail,[10]   10

I'll do, I'll do, and I'll do.[11]

---

1 (Samuel Johnson remarks, "Witches seem to have been most suspected of malice against swine"; quoted in Furness, *"Macbeth,"* 31, n. 4)

2 where thou? = where have you been?

3 piggishly: the sailor's wife is described, two lines below, as "rump-fed," hind quarters of beef being, then and now, relatively choice cuts; the wife's "rump" is clearly well fed

4 said, declared (witches demand, they do not request, and they are rarely if ever polite)

5 go away

6 pampered/overfed female

7 Syrian port city

8 captain

9 (common waterborne vehicle for witches and other supernaturally endowed creatures)

10 (an imperfectly understood detail, for which there are assorted explanations: witches cannot transform themselves into body parts lacking to them as women; the witch flaunts the fact that, unlike a rat, she does not need a tail as a rudder; the witch does not even need paws – so why bother creating a tail?)

11 (intoned, with a gleeful malice)

Witch 2 I'll give thee a wind.[12]

Witch 1 Th'rt[13] kind.

Witch 3 And I another.[14]

15 *Witch 1* I myself have[15] all the other,[16]

And the very[17] ports they blow,[18]

All the quarters[19] that they know[20]

I' the shipman's card.[21]

I'll drain him dry as hay.

20 Sleep shall neither night nor day

Hang upon his penthouse lid.[22]

He shall live a man forbid,[23]

Weary sev'n nights nine times nine[24]

Shall he dwindle,[25] peak,[26] and pine.[27]

---

12 at her back: witches could control winds ("wind" rhymes with "blind / find / hind")

13 thou art

14 another wind

15 control

16 the other winds

17 true, reliable

18 they blow = to which they blow

19 the four quarters of the compass: North, South, East, and West

20 (1) list, set out, (2) are familiar with, have learned by heart

21 chart

22 penthouse lid = eyelid(s) (so called because the eyelids slope down from the front of the house, like – in French – *une appentis,* or lean-to building / roof, adjoining a house)

23 accursed

24 (see below at note 39; because the apostrophe, here, "eliminates" the second syllable of "seven," the line is prosodically scanned, but *not* pronounced: WEAry SEV nights NINE times NINE; this is a poetic convention, not a linguistic / language one)

25 waste away

26 shrink, mope

27 (1) suffer (feel "pain"), (2) be consumed / emaciated

Though his bark cannot be lost,[28]   25
Yet it shall be tempest tossed.[29]
Look what I have.
Witch 2 Show me, show me.
Witch 1 Here I have a pilot's thumb,[30]
Wrecked[31] as homeward he did come.   30

DRUM[32] WITHIN

Witch 3 A drum, a drum!
Macbeth doth come.
All   The weyward[33] sisters,[34] hand in hand,[35]
Posters[36] of the sea and land,
Thus do go about, about.   35
Thrice to thine[37] and thrice to mine,[38]

---

28 cannot be lost: an unexplained limitation on the witch's power, though
   Shakespeare and his audience probably knew its source and reasons for being
29 YET it SHALL be TEMpest TOSSED
30 pilot's thumb = steersman's/helmsman's severed thumb (see act 1, scene 1,
   note 3)
31 shipwrecked
32 there is no indication of who is doing the drumming: Macbeth and Banquo
   are unaccompanied
33 weird, supernatural, with power to control fate ("wyrd," in Old English,
   meant "fate, destiny": "weyward," used in the 1613 Folio text, probably stems
   from a dialectal variation, "weyard," still common in parts of the English-
   speaking world)
34 members of a female order/group (the classical three sisters, the Parcae, or
   Fates, were known as "the three sisters")
35 (i.e., they are dancing in a witches' circle/ring: this is a necessary magical
   rite, not entertainment: they are "winding up" – as one winds up a clock or a
   spring motor – their spell/charm)
36 swift-traveling persons
37 to one side, right or left
38 to the other side, left or right

And thrice again, to make up nine.[39]

Peace:[40] the charm's wound up.

ENTER MACBETH AND BANQUO

Macbeth So foul and fair a day[41] I have not seen.

40 *Banquo* How far is't called[42] to Forres? (*sees Witches*) What are these,

So withered[43] and so wild[44] in their attire,

That look not like th' inhabitants o' the earth,

And yet are on't? (*to Witches*) Live you? Or are you aught

That man may question? You seem to understand me,

45 By each at once her choppy[45] finger laying

Upon her skinny[46] lips. You should[47] be women,

And yet your beards forbid[48] me to interpret[49]

That you are so.

Macbeth   Speak, if you can. What[50] are you?

Witch 1 All hail,[51] Macbeth, hail to thee, Thane of Glamis![52]

---

39 (three being a magic number, three times three is still more potent)
40 be silent/still★
41 (1) the day has been fair in matters military but foul in its weather, (2) a fair day has been changed to a foul one, probably by the witches' magic
42 said to be
43 shriveled, shrunken
44 strange, fantastic
45 having cracked/fissured skin
46 lean, emaciated
47 ought to, must
48 stop, restrain
49 understand
50 (1) what kind of creature, (2) who
51 literally "We wish you all health," this is a traditional greeting/salutation, so well known and established that that it was used as a noun, as in "an all hail," "the all hail"★
52 Macbeth's present title and estates (by inheritance, at the death of his father) (all HAIL macBETH hail TO thee THANE of GLAmis)

Witch 2   All hail, Macbeth, hail to thee, Thane of Cawdor![53]   50

Witch 3   All hail, Macbeth, that shalt be king hereafter!

Banquo   Good sir, why do you start,[54] and seem to fear
    Things that do sound so fair? (*to Witches*) In th' name of truth,
    Are ye fantastical,[55] or that indeed
    Which outwardly ye show?[56] My noble partner[57]   55
    You greet with present grace[58] and great[59] prediction
    Of noble having and of royal hope,
    That he seems rapt withal.[60] To me you speak not.
    If you can look into the seeds of time
    And say which grain will grow and which will not,   60
    Speak then to me, who neither beg nor fear
    Your favors nor your hate.

Witch 1   Hail.

Witch 2   Hail.

Witch 3   Hail.   65

Witch 1   Lesser than Macbeth, and greater.

Witch 2   Not so happy, yet much happier.

Witch 3   Thou shalt get[61] kings, though thou be none.
    So all hail, Macbeth and Banquo!

Witch 1   Banquo and Macbeth, all hail!   70

Macbeth   Stay,[62] you imperfect[63] speakers, tell me more.

53 higher title and estates currently held by another man
54 act/appear visibly startled
55 imaginary★
56 seem, appear
57 associate, companion★
58 present grace = instant/quick goodwill/favor
59 large, important
60 rapt withal = enraptured★ by/with
61 beget, procreate
62 (1) halt, stop, (2) remain
63 unfinished, incomplete

By Sinel's[64] death I know I am[65] Thane of Glamis,
But how of Cawdor? The Thane of Cawdor lives,
A prosperous[66] gentleman, and to be king

75   Stands[67] not within the prospect[68] of belief,
No more than to be Cawdor. Say from whence
You owe[69] this strange intelligence?[70] Or why
Upon this blasted[71] heath you stop our way[72]
With such prophetic greeting? Speak, I charge[73] you.

WITCHES VANISH

80   *Banquo*   The earth hath bubbles, as the water has,
And these are of them. Whither are they vanished?[74]
Macbeth Into the air, and what seemed corporal[75] melted
As breath into the wind. Would[76] they had stayed.
Banquo   Were such things here as we do speak about?

85   Or have we eaten on the insane root[77]
That takes the reason[78] prisoner?
Macbeth Your children shall[79] be kings.

64 (his father)
65 I'm (?)
66 flourishing, thriving
67 is, exists
68 outlook, appearance, expectation
69 have, possess
70 strange intelligence = astonishing/singular/queer knowledge
71 blighted, parched
72 path, road★
73 command, order
74 and THESE are OF them WHIther ARE they VANished
75 to have a body, to be bodily in nature★ (inTO the AIR and WHAT seemed CORPril MELted)
76 I wish, if only
77 on the insane root = of the insanity-causing herb/plant
78 mind
79 (meaning both "will" and "must")★

Banquo   You shall be king.

Macbeth And Thane of Cawdor too. Went it not so?

Banquo To the selfsame[80] tune and words. Who's here?[81]

ENTER ROSS AND ANGUS

Ross   The king hath happily received, Macbeth,   90
      The news of thy success, and when he reads[82]
      Thy personal[83] venture in the rebels' fight,
      His wonders[84] and his praises do contend[85]
      Which should be thine or his.[86] Silenced with that,[87]
      In viewing o'er[88] the rest o' the selfsame day,   95
      He finds thee in the stout[89] Norweyan ranks,
      Nothing[90] afeard of what thyself didst make,[91]
      Strange images[92] of death. As thick as hail[93]
      Came post with post,[94] and every one did bear
      Thy praises in his kingdom's great defense,   100
      And poured them down before him.

80 identical
81 TO the SELFsame TUNE and WORDS who's HERE
82 thinks about, considers
83 (1) individual, (2) bodily
84 astonishment, admiration
85 fight, compete★
86 both the king's admiration/wonder and his desire to praise Macbeth are so
    strong and evenly balanced that Duncan is unsure which does or should
    come first
87 with that = by that struggle/uncertainty
88 viewing o'er = considering, scrutinizing
89 fierce, resolute, brave
90 not at all★
91 produce, be the cause of, create
92 forms, copies, representations (Macbeth was creating corpses)
93 (the 1623 Folio text has "tale," but the closest that comes to making sense is
    "tally" or "complete enumeration")
94 post with post = message/message bearers, one after the other (all coming to
    the king)

Angus   We are sent
        To give thee from our royal master thanks,
        Only to herald[95] thee into his sight,
        Not pay thee.
Ross   And, for an earnest[96] of a greater honor,
105   He bade me, from him, call thee Thane of Cawdor –
        In which addition,[97] hail, most worthy Thane,
        For it is thine.
Banquo   What, can the devil speak true?[98]
Macbeth The Thane of Cawdor lives. Why do you dress me
        In borrowed robes?
Angus   Who was the Thane lives yet,
110   But under heavy judgment[99] bears that life
        Which he deserves to lose. Whether he was combined[100]
        With those of Norway, or did line[101] the rebel
        With hidden help and vantage,[102] or that with both
        He labored in his country's wrack,[103] I know not,
115   But treasons capital,[104] confessed and proved,
        Have overthrown him.
Macbeth   (*aside*) Glamis, and Thane of Cawdor.

95 usher
96 installment, foretaste, pledge★
97 (1) title, style of address, (2) incremental honor
98 reliably, honestly, truthfully (this may well be spoken aside, only for
    Macbeth's ears)
99 heavy judgment = serious/grave sentence/punishment
100 allied (which HE deSERVES to LOSE WHEther he WAS comBINED—
    hexameter, a meter used over and over in this play)
101 strengthen, reinforce
102 benefit, advantage
103 damage, destruction, ruin★
104 punishable by death (adjective modifying "treasons")

The greatest is behind.[105] (*to Ross and Angus*) Thanks for your
pains.[106]

(*to Banquo*) Do you not hope your children shall be kings,
When those[107] that gave[108] the Thane of Cawdor to me
Promised no less to them?[109]

Banquo   (*aside to Macbeth*) That trusted
   home[110]   120
Might yet enkindle[111] you unto the crown,
Besides the Thane of Cawdor. But 'tis strange.
And oftentimes, to win[112] us to our harm,
The instruments[113] of darkness tell us truths,
Win us with honest[114] trifles, to betray's[115]   125
In deepest consequence.[116]

   (*to Ross and Angus*) Cousins, a word, I pray you.

Macbeth   (*aside*) Two
   truths are told,
As happy prologues to the swelling act[117]

---

105 the greatest is behind = (1) the largest step has been accomplished, (2) the
   greatest achievement will/can now follow
106 trouble, labor★
107 those persons (the witches)
108 (1) indicated, showed, told, portrayed, (2) bestowed
109 to Banquo's children
110 as far as it will go
111 enkindle you = inflame/excite you toward ("unto")
112 entice, persuade
113 agents
114 truthful
115 betray us
116 deepest consequence = the most serious/awful/solemn subsequent event/
   sequel
117 swelling act = growing/expanding outcome/action

Of the imperial theme.[118] — (*to Ross and Angus*) I thank you,
gentlemen.

130   (*aside*) This supernatural soliciting[119]
Cannot be ill,[120] cannot be good. If ill,
Why hath it given me earnest of success,
Commencing in a truth? I am[121] Thane of Cawdor.
If good, why do I yield to that suggestion[122]

135   Whose horrid image doth unfix my hair[123]
And make my seated[124] heart knock at my ribs,
Against the use[125] of nature?[126] Present fears
Are less than horrible imaginings.
My thought, whose murder[127] yet is but fantastical,

140   Shakes so my single state of man[128] that function[129]
Is smothered[130] in surmise,[131] and nothing is
But what is not.

Banquo   (*to Ross and Angus*) Look, how our partner's
rapt.

Macbeth (*aside*) If chance will have me king, why, chance may
crown me,

118 the imperial theme = the subject/matter of sovereign rule
119 encitement, stimulation (with negative connotations) (this SUperNAturAL soLIciTING)
120 bad, wicked
121 I'm (?)
122 (1) temptation, (2) intention, (3) deceitful statement
123 unfix my hair = make my hair stand on end
124 fixed, firmly placed (as opposed to his hair?)
125 customary practice
126 of nature = (1) of human beings, (2) of Macbeth in particular
127 act of murder (of the king)
128 single state of man = individual condition as a man ("my very being")
129 movement, activity
130 (1) suppressed, repressed, (2) suffocated
131 conjectures, conceptions, imaginings

Without my stir.[132]

Banquo　　　　　　　(*to Ross and Angus*) New honors come[133]
　　upon him,
　　Like our strange[134] garments, cleave[135] not to their mold　　145
　　But[136] with the aid of use.

Macbeth　　　　　　　(*aside*) Come what come may,[137]
　　Time and the hour[138] runs through the roughest[139] day.

Banquo　Worthy Macbeth, we stay[140] upon your leisure.

Macbeth　Give me your favor.[141] My dull brain was wrought[142]
　　With things forgotten.[143] Kind gentlemen, your pains　　150
　　Are registered[144] where every day I turn
　　The leaf to read them.[145] Let us toward[146] the king.
　　(*to Banquo*) Think upon what hath chanced,[147] and at more
　　time,[148]
　　The interim[149] having weighed[150] it, let us speak

132 actively doing anything
133 that have come
134 unfamiliar
135 adhere, stick fast
136 except, only
137 come WHAT come MAY
138 time and the hour = time (in general) and the present moment
139 harshest, most disagreeable
140 tarry, wait*
141 indulgence, pardon
142 agitated
143 (1) things he is trying to recall, (2) things he has forgotten to do
144 duly recorded
145 (i.e., in his mind)
146 go onward toward
147 happened
148 at more time = at some later point, after a while
149 intervening period
150 balanced, considered, assessed, judged

Our free[151] hearts each to other.

155 *Banquo*   Very gladly.

    Macbeth Till then, enough. (*to the others*) Come, friends.

EXEUNT

---

151 unrestricted, unrestrained

SCENE 4
Forres. The king's palace

FLOURISH.[1] ENTER DUNCAN, MALCOLM, DONALBAIN, LENNOX, AND SERVANTS

Duncan Is execution[2] done on Cawdor? Are not
Those in commission[3] yet returned?

Malcolm   My liege,[4]
They are not yet come back. But I have spoke
With one that saw him die, who did report
That very frankly[5] he confessed his treasons,   5
Implored your highness' pardon and set forth[6]
A deep repentance. Nothing in his life
Became[7] him like the leaving it: he died
As one[8] that[9] had been studied[10] in his death
To throw away the dearest[11] thing he owed,[12]   10
As 'twere[13] a careless[14] trifle.

---

1 fanfare
2 carrying out of sentence/punishment
3 in commission = in charge, given the duty/responsibility
4 (in Shakespeare's England, used as a short form of "my liege lord" – i.e., "my feudal lord/superior")
5 freely, unconditionally, openly
6 set forth = expressed, declared
7 suited, was proper for, looked well on
8 as one = like someone
9 who
10 deliberate, intentionally intending, carefully prepared
11 best, most cherished
12 owned★
13 as 'twere = as if it were
14 unimportant, insignificant

Duncan   There is no art[15]
  To find[16] the mind's construction[17] in the face.
  He was a gentleman on whom I built[18]
  An absolute trust.

  ENTER MACBETH, BANQUO, ROSS, AND ANGUS

                    (*to Macbeth*) O worthiest cousin,
15   The sin of my ingratitude even now[19]
    Was heavy on me. Thou art so far before[20]
    That[21] swiftest wing[22] of recompense[23] is slow
    To overtake[24] thee. Would thou hadst less deserved,
    That[25] the proportion[26] both of thanks and payment
20   Might have been mine.[27] Only[28] I have[29] left to say,
    More is thy due than more than all can pay.[30]

---

15 human skill/learning/method
16 discover, perceive, recognize
17 logic, nature
18 established, formed
19 even now = just now
20 ahead★ ("out in front" in the sense, here, of "superior")
21 that the
22 means of flight
23 reward, compensation/payment
24 catch up to
25 so that
26 comparative relation/balance between
27 that THE proPORtion BOTH of THANKS and PAYment / MIGHT have
   been MINE (note: [1] prosodic movement does not necessarily end when a
   printed line does, [2] inversion of stress is most frequent in the first metrical
   foot of a line, as here: MIGHT have)
28 all
29 I've (?)
30 ("you are owed more than everything I can give you could properly reward
   you for")

Macbeth The service[31] and the loyalty I owe,

In doing it pays itself.[32] Your highness' part[33]

Is to receive our duties,[34] and our duties

Are, to your throne and state,[35] children and servants,   25

Which do but[36] what they should, by doing everything

Safe toward[37] your love and honor.

Duncan   Welcome hither.

I have begun to plant[38] thee, and will labor

To make thee full of[39] growing. Noble Banquo,

That[40] hast no less deserved, nor must be known   30

No less to have done so,[41] let me enfold[42] thee

And hold thee to my heart.

Banquo   There if I grow,

The harvest is your own.

Duncan   (*weeping*) My plenteous joys,

Wanton[43] in fulness, seek to hide themselves

In drops of sorrow. Sons, kinsmen, thanes,[44]   35

31 obligations (of someone who serves/has sworn allegiance to someone else)
32 ("pays itself in doing it")
33 share, portion
34 our duties = the actions we owe you
35 status, rank★
36 simply
37 safe toward = protective of
38 establish, position, place (verb)
39 full of = abundant in, replete with
40 who
41 no LESS to HAVE done SO
42 clasp, embrace
43 ungovernable, unruly
44 SONS KINSmen THANES

And you whose places[45] are the nearest,[46] know
We[47] will establish our estate upon[48]
Our eldest, Malcolm, whom we name hereafter[49]
The Prince of Cumberland,[50] which honor must
40   Not unaccompanied[51] invest him only,[52]
But signs[53] of nobleness, like stars, shall[54] shine
On all deservers. From hence to Inverness,[55]
And bind us further[56] to you.

Macbeth The rest[57] is labor,[58] which is not used[59] for you.
45   I'll be myself the harbinger[60] and make joyful
The hearing of my wife[61] with your approach.[62]
So humbly take my leave.

Duncan   My worthy Cawdor.

45 rank, status, position
46 most closely connected to the king, because of intimacy or kinship
47 the royal "we" = "I"
48 establish our estate upon = ordain that my title, powers, and possessions will
    be inherited by
49 in accordance with this decree ("from now on")
50 title which, in Scotland, created someone as heir to the throne (kingship not
    being automatically inherited)
51 not unaccompanied = not alone
52 invest him only = envelop/clothe only him
53 marks, tokens
54 must and will
55 from hence to Inverness = let us all now proceed from here to Inverness (site
    of Macbeth's castle)
56 and bind us further = where/so that I may still more tie/fasten/unite myself
    and you
57 the rest = what remains (still to be done)
58 exertion, physical activity
59 customary, usual, proper (adjective)
60 somone sent in advance ("forerunner")★
61 ("my wife's hearing")
62 coming, drawing near

Duncan converses with Banquo

Macbeth (*aside*) The Prince of Cumberland. That is a step[63]
    On which I must fall down, or else o'erleap,
    For in my way it lies. Stars, hide your fires,[64]   50
    Let not light see my black and deep desires,
    The eye[65] wink[66] at the hand. Yet let that be[67]
    Which the eye fears, when it is done, to see.

EXIT MACBETH

Duncan True, worthy Banquo. He is full so valiant,[68]
    And in his commendations[69] I am fed.[70]   55
    It is a banquet to me. Let's[71] after him,
    Whose care[72] is gone before to bid us welcome.
    It[73] is a peerless[74] kinsman.

FLOURISH. EXEUNT

63 (1) action, (2) stair (and also, perhaps, a reference to a move in chess)
64 visible light (stars HIDE your FIRES)
65 the eye = let/may the eye ("eye" here carrying the sense of "mind, reason" –
    and also of "conscience")
66 act as if it does not see, connive at
67 happen, come to pass
68 full so valiant = so completely courageous/stouthearted/brave (true
    WORthy BANquo HE is FULL so VALiant)
69 his commendations = praising him
70 gratified, sustained, comforted
71 let us go
72 whose care = he whose concern/solicitude (i.e., Macbeth)
73 he
74 matchless, incomparable, unequaled

SCENE 5

Inverness.[1] Macbeth's castle.

ENTER LADY MACBETH, READING A LETTER

Lady Macbeth "They[2] met me in[3] the day of success.[4] And
I have learned, by the perfectest[5] report, they have more in
them than mortal knowledge. When I burned in desire to
question them further, they made themselves air, into which
they vanished. Whiles I stood rapt in the wonder of it, came
missives[6] from the king, who all hailed me 'Thane of
Cawdor,' by which title, before, these weird sisters saluted[7]
me, and referred me[8] to the coming on of time, with 'Hail,
king that shalt be!' This have I thought good to deliver[9] thee,
my dearest partner of greatness, that thou mightst not lose the
dues[10] of rejoicing, by being ignorant of what greatness is
promised thee. Lay[11] it to thy heart, and farewell."

Glamis thou art, and Cawdor, and shalt be
What thou art promised. Yet do I fear thy nature:
It is too full o' the milk of human kindness[12]

1 central Scotland, roughly 100 mi. N of Glasgow
2 the witches
3 on
4 military/battle success
5 (1) fullest, most complete, (2) faultless, most certain
6 messengers
7 addressed, greeted
8 referred me = directed/pointed me
9 transmit/report/communicate to
10 (1) right, (2) that which is owed
11 deposit, place, set
12 It has been suggested that this should be, in effect, one word: "humankind-
    ness." The 1623 Folio's spelling, used in this edition, does not at first seem to
    settle the issue, since "kindness" then meant "kinship." But the *OED*'s earliest

To catch[13] the nearest[14] way. Thou wouldst[15] be great,
Art not without ambition, but without
The illness[16] should attend[17] it. What thou wouldst highly,[18]
That wouldst thou holily, wouldst not play false,
And yet wouldst wrongly[19] win. Thou'dst[20] have, great   20
Glamis,
That which cries[21] "Thus thou must do" if thou have[22] it,
And[23] that which rather[24] thou dost fear to do
Than wishest should be undone. Hie[25] thee hither,
That I may pour my spirits[26] in thine ear,
And chastise[27] with the valor of my tongue   25
All that impedes thee from the golden round,[28]
Which fate and metaphysical[29] aid doth seem
To have thee crowned withal.

---

citation for "humankind" is approximately 1645. This too is not conclusive.
Yet a metaphor based on mother's milk seems to fit a good deal better with
the more traditional reading, and "kindness" as "the state of being kind" is
cited in the *OED* from about 1350 on. The *OED* editors cite "the milk of
human kindness" as one among the citations for "the quality or habit of
being kind"
13 seize, lay hold / take possession of
14 most direct / shortest
15 want to
16 wickedness, depravity
17 should attend = that ought to accompany★
18 very much, greatly
19 unjustly, unfittingly
20 you would / wish / want to
21 calls out / begs
22 are / want to have
23 and on the other hand / at the same time
24 more
25 hasten, hurry★
26 vital powers / character / disposition
27 discipline, reform, correct
28 the golden round = the kingly crown
29 supernatural

ENTER A MESSENGER

What is your tidings?

Messenger   The king comes here tonight.

Lady Macbeth   Thou'rt mad[30] to
say it.

30   Is not thy master with him? – who, were't so,
Would have informed for[31] preparation.[32]

Messenger   So please you, it is true. Our thane is coming.
One of my fellows[33] had the speed of[34] him,
Who, almost dead for breath,[35] had scarcely more[36]

35   Than would make up[37] his message.

Lady Macbeth   Give him tending,[38]
He brings great news.

EXIT MESSENGER

The raven himself[39] is hoarse,
That[40] croaks the fatal[41] entrance of Duncan
Under my[42] battlements. Come, you spirits
That tend on[43] mortal thoughts, unsex me here,

30 frenzied, delusional, insane
31 informed me for the purpose of making
32 PREpaRAtiON
33 colleagues, comrades
34 the speed of = a faster rate of progression (by running) than
35 shortness of breath
36 more breath left
37 would make up = constituted, formed
38 care, attention
39 indeed, in fact
40 he who (the raven being a singularly appropriate announcer of Duncan's ill-
    fated visit)
41 fated, destined to bring doom★
42 (not "these battlements," or "Macbeth's," or even "Macbeth's and my," but "my")
43 tend on = watch over, take charge of, wait upon ("attend to")

And fill me, from the crown[44] to the toe, top full[45]   40
Of direst[46] cruelty! Make thick[47] my blood,
Stop up the access and passage[48] to remorse,[49]
That no compunctious visitings[50] of nature
Shake my fell purpose,[51] nor keep peace between
The effect[52] and it. Come to my woman's breasts   45
And take[53] my milk for[54] gall,[55] you murd'ring ministers,[56]
Wherever[57] in your sightless[58] substances[59]
You wait on[60] nature's mischief![61] Come, thick night,[62]
And pall[63] thee in the dunnest[64] smoke of hell,
That my keen[65] knife see not the wound it makes,   50

44 top of the head★
45 top full = brim full, filled to the very top
46 most horrible/terrible/evil
47 dense (so sentiments *not* cruel – e.g., pity – cannot flow to her heart)
48 access and passage = entrance and (1) transit, (2) right/opportunity of
    movement
49 to remorse = do not allow "access and passage" to (1) regret, repentance,
    conscience, (2) pity/compassion/tenderness
50 compunctious visitings = remorseful influences
51 fell purpose = fierce/savage/cruel intention/resolution★
52 result
53 accept, receive
54 in exchange for
55 liver bile, traditionally associated with bitterness, rancor, etc.
56 agents★
57 (i.e., "come" from "wherever" you "wait on")
58 invisible, unseen, dark
59 essences, essential natures
60 wait on = wait for, await
61 evil, misfortune, misery
62 (Wills, *Witches and Jesuits,* 56, cites the "begetter" of *Macbeth,* King James,
    who wrote in his *Daemonologie* that the devil can "thicken and obscure the
    air . . . that the beams of any other man's eye cannot pierce through the same
    to see them")
63 cover, drape
64 darkest, murkiest, gloomiest
65 exceedingly sharp

Nor heaven peep through the blanket of the dark,
To cry "Hold, hold."[66]

ENTER MACBETH

                 Great Glamis, worthy Cawdor,
Greater than both, by the all-hail hereafter,[67]
Thy letters have transported me beyond
55   This ignorant[68] present, and I feel now
The future in the instant.[69]
Macbeth   My dearest love,
Duncan comes here tonight.
Lady Macbeth   And when goes hence?
Macbeth Tomorrow, as he purposes.[70]
Lady Macbeth   O, never
Shall[71] sun that morrow[72] see.
60   Your face, my thane, is as a book where men
May read strange[73] matters. To beguile[74] the time,[75]
Look like the time, bear welcome in your eye,
Your hand, your tongue. Look like the innocent flower,[76]
But be the serpent under't. He that's coming

66 stop
67 of/about time to come/the future
68 uninformed, unknowing
69 present, this moment
70 intends, plans★
71 must
72 morning★
73 unknown, astonishing
74 deceive, delude
75 the time = the age, the present★
76 look LIKE the INnocent FLOWer (the two unstressed vowels in "innocent"
   are reduced: not /inohsent/ but /inisənt/

Must be provided[77] for, and you shall[78] put   65
This night's great business[79] into my dispatch,[80]
Which shall[81] to all our nights and days to come
Give solely[82] sovereign sway and masterdom.

Macbeth   We will speak further.

Lady Macbeth   Only look up clear.[83]
To alter favor[84] ever is[85] to fear.[86]   70
Leave all the rest to me.

EXEUNT

77 provided for = prepared/gotten ready for
78 must
79 task, labor, job
80 (noun) (1) management, (2) putting to death, killing by violence (a chilling pun)
81 shall . . . give = will give (the auxiliary form of "shall"; Renaissance English fluctuates between the word's two meanings, though only the auxiliary form is – barely – alive today)
82 alone, exclusively
83 look up clear = be cheerful/bright/serene/innocent* seeming
84 appearance, countenance/face
85 ever is = is always
86 (1) to be afraid, (2) to show that fear to others

SCENE 6

Before Macbeth's castle

HAUTBOYS[1] AND TORCHES.[2] ENTER DUNCAN, MALCOLM,
DONALBAIN, BANQUO, LENNOX, MACDUFF, ROSS,
ANGUS, AND SERVANTS

Duncan This castle hath a pleasant seat.[3] The air
    Nimbly[4] and sweetly recommends itself
    Unto our gentle[5] senses.

Banquo   This guest of summer,
    The temple-haunting[6] martlet,[7] does approve,[8]
5   By his loved mansionry,[9] that the heaven's breath
    Smells wooingly[10] here. No[11] jutty, frieze,[12]

1 oboes (which can take on a piercing, brassy quality, like trumpets)
2 it is not yet night, but soon will be; further, they are entering a medieval
  castle which, by evening, was a rather dark place – and when they had made
  their entrance, the torches would be set in holders on the castle walls, being
  more effective as general lighting than candles
3 location, situation, site
4 quickly
5 soothed
6 temple haunting = sacred building frequenting
7 a bird (swallow, swift) that builds its nest in masonry, walls, etc.
8 prove, show to be true
9 building/construction in stone
10 alluringly, enticingly
11 no [part of a structure].... but this bird hath = there is no [part of a
  structure] ... where this bird has not
12 (The first 10 lines are all, except for this one, unusually regular. This is of
  course a play, not a sonnet; there are no more or less absolute formal and
  metrical "rules." But iambic pentameter smoothness fits these 10 lines'
  notably contrastive substance and tone – and though it is far more likely that
  this sixth line in the sequence is an iambic tetrameter line, it is perhaps just
  barely possible, considering the word's probable Italian origin, that "frieze,"
  now pronounced monosyllabically [homophonic with "freeze"], was then
  something like FERiyAYze, making this line, too, iambic pentameter)

Buttress, nor coign[13] of vantage,[14] but this bird
Hath made his pendent[15] bed and procreant cradle.[16]
Where they most breed and haunt,[17] I have observed,
The air is delicate.[18]

ENTER LADY MACBETH

Duncan   See, see, our honored hostess![19]   10
(*to Lady Macbeth*) The love that follows us[20] sometime is our trouble,[21]
Which still we thank[22] as love. Herein I teach[23] you
How you shall bid[24] God 'ield us[25] for your pains,
And thank us[26] for your trouble.

Lady Macbeth   All our service,[27]
In every point[28] twice done and then done double,   15

---

13 (1) jutty, (2) frieze, (3) buttress, . . . (4) coign = (1) projecting part of a building, (2) decorated/sculptured slab resting on a column, (3) structure supporting a wall/building from the outside, (4) projecting corner/angle of a building
14 of vantage = useful
15 overhanging, slanting
16 procreant cradle = baby-producing little bed
17 (verb) are regularly/usually found
18 delightful, pleasant
19 see SEE our HONored HOSTess
20 follows us = serves/attends upon/pursues me (the royal "we")
21 affliction, distress, vexation
22 are grateful for
23 show, make known to, instruct
24 shall bid = ought to entreat/pray to/ask★
25 'ield us for your pains = to reward ("'ield" = "yield") me on account of the trouble you experience
26 thank us = be grateful to me (i.e., because Duncan, the king, is thus demonstrating his "love" for her)
27 attendance on our master and lord, the king
28 were it in every item/part

Were poor and single[29] business to contend
Against those honors deep and broad wherewith
Your Majesty loads our house.[30] For those of old,[31]
And the late dignities[32] heaped up to them,[33]
We rest your hermits.[34]

20 *Duncan*   Where's the Thane of Cawdor?
We coursed[35] him at the heels, and had a purpose
To be his purveyor.[36] But he rides well,
And his great love,[37] sharp as his spur, hath holp[38] him
To his home before us. Fair and noble hostess,
We are your guest tonight.

25 *Lady Macbeth*   Your servants ever
Have theirs, themselves, and what is theirs, in compt,[39]
To make their audit[40] at your highness' pleasure,[41]

---

29 single business = scanty/plain/slight/trivial activity/work
30 (1) home, (2) the inmates/family living in a home
31 those of old = former honors
32 late dignities = recent honors
33 heaped up to them = piled just as high as the former honors
34 rest your hermits = remain your beneficiaries who, like pensioners,
   almsmen, and other poor folk, are charged with praying for the souls of their
   benefactors (they were thus "beadsmen" – those who pray for others'
   salvation – a term that included licensed beggars)
35 rode after, pursued
36 provider (who rose in advance of a traveling king, to ensure that all the royal
   needs would be satisfied: the king deliberately pretends to reverse roles with
   Macbeth, in his host's honor)
37 (for Lady Macbeth)
38 helped
39 in compt = on account (an interim payment, held only until some final
   settlement of accounts)
40 detailed verification of accounts
41 at your ... pleasure = whenever you wish/please

Still[42] to return your own.[43]
Duncan   Give me your hand.
Conduct me to mine host: we love him highly,
And shall continue our graces[44] towards him.   30
By your leave,[45] hostess.

EXEUNT

42 always ("still" and "ever," meaning the same thing, here reinforce one
    another)
43 your own = that which belongs to you (in medieval law, everything
    belonged to the king, who could in theory and, sometimes, in practice,
    reclaim "his own" at his pleasure)
44 honors, favors
45 by your leave = with your permission (a courteous way of suggesting that it
    was up to her, as hostess, to decide if, as the king pleased, they would now
    enter the castle)

SCENE 7

Macbeth's castle

HAUTBOYS AND TORCHES. ENTER A SEWER,[1] AND DIVERS
SERVANTS WITH DISHES AND SERVICE,[2] AND PASS OVER[3]
THE STAGE. THEN ENTER MACBETH

Macbeth If it were done when 'tis done, then 'twere well
 It were done quickly. If th' assassination[4]
 Could trammel up[5] the consequence,[6] and catch
 With his surcease success,[7] that but this blow[8]
5 Might be the be-all and the end-all – here,
 But[9] here, upon this bank and shoal[10] of time,
 We'd jump[11] the life to come. But in these cases

1 head servant, butler, steward
2 food and utensils
3 across, to the other side of
4 killing, by treacherous violence
5 trammel up = bind/fasten up (as [1] in a fish or bird net, [2] devices for
 restraining horses' legs)
6 events/conditions following the murder
7 catch with his surcease success = capture/lay hold of success (1) by means of
 the restraint placed upon the event's "consequence" ("his surcease" meaning
 "the restraint placed upon consequence"), *or* (2) because of his – i.e.,
 Duncan's – death (the latter is a more common reading, today, but the
 former seems more accurate: "surcease" is not elsewhere used to signify
 death, and the *OED* cites the use of the word in *Macbeth*, after explaining
 that "surcease" is most often used to mean "a temporary cessation,
 suspension, or intermission"; further, "catch with his surcease success" is
 preceded by the conjunctive "and," thus making more effective sense of
 "trammeling up consequence")
8 that but this blow = so that this blow only
9 just, right, exactly
10 bank/bar, shallow
11 (1) pass directly to/evade/skip, with no intermediate stages, *or* (2) risk (the
 latter is, again, a more common reading today, but the former makes better
 sense in terms of attaining "the be all and the end all")

We still[12] have judgment here,[13] that we but[14] teach[15]
Bloody instructions,[16] which, being taught,[17] return
To plague the inventor.[18] This even-handed justice   10
Commends[19] the ingredients of our poisoned chalice[20]
To our own lips. He's[21] here in double trust:
First, as I am his kinsman and his subject
(Strong[22] both against the deed), then, as his host,[23]
Who should against his murderer shut the door,   15
Not bear the knife myself. Besides, this Duncan
Hath borne his faculties so meek,[24] hath been
So clear[25] in his great office,[26] that his virtues
Will plead like angels, trumpet tongued,[27] against
The deep damnation[28] of his taking off,[29]   20
And pity, like a naked newborn babe[30]

12 always
13 in these cases we still have judgment here = in such events/deeds, we always have God's judgment here on earth
14 that we but = so that we simply
15 show, present
16 knowledge
17 shown, presented
18 originator, deviser
19 presents, delivers
20 drinking cup
21 (Duncan)
22 strong arguments
23 (the responsibilities of both "host" and "guest," but especially those of the host, were traditionally taken most seriously)
24 borne his faculties so meek = carried his powers so courteously/indulgently/kindly
25 serene, unclouded, unstained, pure
26 position, place, employment, duty*
27 trumpet tongued = as powerfully loud as trumpets
28 damnable sin
29 taking off = departure from this world
30 "Shakespeare's babe is not the Christ child," notes Garry Wills, *Witches and*

Striding[31] the blast,[32] or heaven's cherubim, horsed[33]
Upon the sightless couriers[34] of the air,
Shall blow[35] the horrid deed in every eye,
25 That[36] tears shall drown the wind.[37] I have no spur[38]
To prick the sides of my intent, but only[39]
Vaulting[40] ambition, which o'erleaps itself
And falls on the other —

ENTER LADY MACBETH

How now! What news?
Lady Macbeth He[41] has almost supped.[42] Why have you left the chamber?
Macbeth Hath he asked for me?
30 *Lady Macbeth* Know you not he has?
Macbeth We will proceed no further in this business.

Jesuits, 134. "It is Pity . . . personified." But Shakespeare says "*like* a newborn babe." Exact identification is exceedingly difficult: one frustrated and hapless critic wrote, in 1891, that "this is pure rant, and intended to be so" (*Variorum,* 98)

31 straddling, bestriding
32 wind
33 mounted (like the newborn babe who rides the wind)
34 sightless couriers = blind messengers (i.e., the wind has no eyes)
35 send a current of air from the mouth (that being, of course, precisely how "news" is carried)
36 so that
37 drown the wind = (1) overpower/overwhelm the roar of the wind, *or* (2) thoroughly wet/steep/soak the wind (since the passage concerns spreading news of the damnable deed, the former seems more likely)
38 literally, a spike or spiked wheel with which a rider can prick a horse's sides and urge more speed; metaphorically, "incentive, motivation"
39 but only = except
40 leaping
41 Duncan
42 eaten supper (i.e., very nearly finished his meal)

He hath honored me, of late, and I have bought[43]
Golden opinions from all sorts of people,
Which would[44] be worn[45] now in their newest gloss,[46]
Not cast aside so soon.

Lady Macbeth   Was the hope drunk[47]   35
Wherein you dressed yourself? Hath it slept since?[48]
And wakes it now, to look so green and pale
At what it did so freely?[49] From this time[50]
Such I account[51] thy love. Art thou afeard
To be the same in thine own act and valor   40
As thou art in desire?[52] Wouldst thou have that
Which thou esteem'st[53] the ornament of life,
And live a coward in thine own esteem,[54]
Letting "I dare not" wait upon[55] "I would,"[56]
Like the poor cat i' the adage?[57]

43 had, gained
44 ought to
45 (as one wears clothing or jewelry)
46 newest gloss = freshest brand new shine
47 inebriated, intoxicated
48 i.e., as a drunk would
49 readily, willingly, without reserve/conditions
50 i.e., from this time forth
51 consider, value, think of
52 (the reference to "desire," following hard on her reference to his love for her, is truly fierce-tongued!)
53 value/regard ★ as
54 opinion, valuation
55 wait upon = linger passively for
56 I would = I wish/want to
57 maxim, proverb (*Le chat aime poisson, mais il n'aime pas mouiller la patte,* "The cat loves fish, but it doesn't like getting its paws wet." Cited in English from about 1250: GLApperson, *The Wordsworth Dictionary of Proverbs* [Hertfordshire, 1993], 88a)

45 *Macbeth*   Prithee,[58] peace.
   I dare do all that may become[59] a man.
   Who dares do more is none.[60]
   Lady Macbeth   What beast was't, then,
   That made you break[61] this enterprise[62] to me?
   When you durst[63] do it, then you were a man,
50 And, to be more[64] than what you were, you would[65]
   Be so much more the man. Nor time nor[66] place
   Did then adhere,[67] and yet you would make both.
   They have made themselves, and that – their fitness[68] now –
   Does unmake you. I have given suck, and know[69]
55 How tender[70] 'tis to love the babe that milks me.
   I would, while it was smiling in my face,
   Have plucked my nipple from his boneless[71] gums
   And dashed the[72] brains out, had I so sworn as you
   Have done to this.
   Macbeth   If we should fail?
   Lady Macbeth   We fail?

58 I beg/pray thee*
59 be appropriate/fitting/suitable for
60 no man (i.e., either a devil or a creature of supernatural powers)
61 reveal, disclose
62 undertaking
63 dared
64 to be more = in order to be more
65 wished to
66 nor . . . nor = neither . . . nor
67 hang together, harmonize
68 suitability
69 does UNmake YOU i have [i've?] GIVen SUCK and KNOW
70 fine, precious
71 toothless
72 his

But[73] screw your courage to the sticking place,[74]   60
And we'll not fail. When Duncan is asleep —
Whereto the rather shall[75] his day's hard journey
Soundly invite[76] him — his two chamberlains[77]
Will I with wine and wassail[78] so convince[79]
That memory, the warder[80] of the brain,   65
Shall be a fume,[81] and the receipt[82] of reason
A limbeck only.[83] When in swinish sleep
Their drenchèd natures[84] lie as in a death,
What cannot you and I perform[85] upon
The unguarded Duncan? What not put upon[86]   70
His spongy[87] officers, who shall bear the guilt
Of our great quell?[88]

Macbeth   Bring forth men children only,[89]

---

73 but screw = only/just force/tighten/strain
74 sticking place = final and effective point (knot on a bow string, keeping it
   from slipping out of place)
75 whereto the rather shall = to which it is more likely must
76 soundly invite = profoundly/deeply induce/attract
77 chamber/bedroom servants/attendants
78 the drinking of healths/toasts
79 conquer, overcome
80 watchman, guard
81 volatile smoke/vapor
82 receptacle (actively functioning, because it contains "reason")
83 a mere nonfunctional receptacle (limbeck = alembic, a kind of flask used in
   distilling)
84 drenchèd natures = submerged/drowned characters/capacities
85 bring to pass, carry out, execute (the unGUARDed DUNcan WHAT not
   PUT upON)
86 put upon = divert/assign/impose onto ("saddle")
87 moisture soaked, soggy, sodden
88 killing, murder
89 bring FORTH men CHILdren ONly

For thy undaunted mettle[90] should compose[91]
Nothing but males. Will it[92] not be received,[93]
75   When we have marked with blood those sleepy two
Of his own chamber, and used their very[94] daggers,
That they have done't?

Lady Macbeth   Who dares receive it other,[95]
As[96] we shall make our griefs[97] and clamor[98] roar[99]
Upon his death?

Macbeth   I am settled,[100] and bend up[101]
80   Each corporal agent[102] to this terrible feat.[103]
Away,[104] and mock[105] the time with fairest show.[106]
False face must hide what the false heart doth know.

EXEUNT

90 undaunted mettle = intrepid / undismayed temperament / spirit
91 produce, make, put together
92 (i.e., this story of ours)
93 accepted, adopted, approved
94 own
95 differently
96 while, when
97 suffering, distress
98 loud / excited cries
99 (verb)
100 fixed, firm, undeviating
101 bend up = I aim / make myself ready (as one bends a bow before shooting)
102 corporal agent = bodily power / instrument
103 (1) deed, action, (2) crime
104 "let's go"
105 (1) defy, set at nought, (2) deceive, befool
106 display, demonstration (the first line of this concluding rhymed couplet is
    metrically highly regular: aWAY and MOCK the TIME with FAIRest
    SHOW. The second line is almost impossible to scan. Perhaps it is meant to
    run: false FACE must HIDE what THE false HEART doth SHOW, though
    it seems unlikely to have been thus spoken)

Act 2

SCENE I
Court[1] of Macbeth's castle

ENTER BANQUO, AND FLEANCE, BEARING A TORCH
BEFORE HIM

Banquo How goes the night, boy?

Fleance The moon is down, I have not heard the clock.[2]

Banquo And she goes down at twelve.

Fleance   I take't, 'tis later, sir.

Banquo Hold,[3] take my sword. There's husbandry[4] in heaven:

Their candles[5] are all out. Take thee that[6] too.   5

A heavy summons[7] lies like lead upon me,

---

1 outer grounds, yard
2 (watches were not common; people told time by tolling clocks or, during the
   day, by the sun)
3 wait
4 domestic economy
5 (i.e., the stars)
6 (unspecified equipment – shield, dagger, etc.)
7 heavy summons = weighty/intense/profound command/call (to sleep)

And yet I would not[8] sleep. Merciful powers,
Restrain in me the cursèd thoughts that nature
Gives way to, in repose.

enter Macbeth, *and a* Servant *with a torch*

(*to Fleance*) Give me my sword.
Who's there?
10 *Macbeth*   A friend.
Banquo   What, sir, not yet at rest? The king's a-bed:
He hath been in unusual pleasure,[9] and
Sent forth great largess[10] to your offices.[11]
This diamond he greets[12] your wife withal,[13]
15 By the name of most kind hostess, and shut up[14]
In measureless content.
Macbeth   Being unprepared,
Our will became the servant to defect,[15]
Which else[16] should free[17] have wrought.[18]
Banquo   All's well.
I dreamt last night of the three weird sisters:
To you they have[19] showed some[20] truth.

8 do not wish/want to
9 in unusual pleasure = exceptionally/uncommonly pleased
10 munificence, bounty
11 servants (i.e., those who have served – done "offices" – for him)
12 salutes, honors
13 in addition, as well★
14 shut up = he closed/finished/concluded
15 deFECT (noun)
16 otherwise
17 unrestricted, generously★
18 worked, performed
19 they've (?)
20 a degree of

Macbeth   I think not of²¹   20
them.
Yet, when we can entreat²² an hour to serve,²³
We would²⁴ spend it in some words upon that business,²⁵
If you would grant the time.

Banquo   At your kind'st leisure.²⁶

Macbeth If you shall cleave²⁷ to my consent,²⁸ when 'tis,
It shall make honor²⁹ for you.

Banquo   So³⁰ I lose none   25
In seeking to augment it,³¹ but still keep
My bosom franchised³² and allegiance³³ clear,
I shall be counseled.³⁴

Macbeth   Good repose the while.³⁵

Banquo Thanks, sir. The like³⁶ to you.

EXEUNT BANQUO AND FLEANCE

Macbeth Go bid thy mistress, when my drink is ready,³⁷   30

21 about, concerning
22 manage, find
23 satisfy/gratify us, be useful
24 ought to
25 matter, subject, affair
26 kind'st leisure = most agreeable opportunity
27 hold firm, be consistent/faithful
28 proposal
29 credit, distinction, high rank
30 as long as
31 augment it = further/enhance your proposal
32 free (of guilt)
33 my duties/loyalties/obligations to my lord (the king)
34 shall be counseled = am prepared to be advised/directed
35 good repose the while = sleep well meanwhile/in the meantime
36 same
37 (there is no drink in preparation, only a murder; the bell will notify Macbeth
   that they are to proceed)

She strike upon the bell. Get thee to bed.

(*Macbeth, staring*) Is this a dagger which I see before me,
The handle toward my hand?[38] Come,[39] let me clutch[40]
thee.
(*he reaches, in vain*) I have thee not,[41] and yet I see thee still.
35   Art thou not, fatal vision,[42] sensible[43]
To feeling as[44] to sight? Or art thou but[45]
A dagger of the mind, a false[46] creation,
Proceeding[47] from the heat oppressèd[48] brain?
I see thee yet, in form[49] as palpable[50]
40   (*he draws his own dagger*) As this which now I draw.
Thou marshall'st[51] me the way that I was going,
And such[52] an instrument I was[53] to use.

38 (i.e., ready to be grasped)
39 (an encouraging imperative, giving an invitation/encouragement)
40 grasp tightly, with my hand
41 have thee not = do not hold/possess you in my hand
42 fatal vision = fateful/necessary/ominous/deadly (1) sight, (2) sight not
physically apparent
43 perceivable
44 as you are, as well as
45 only★
46 deceptive, deceitful, treacherous, spurious, sham (many critics have suggested
that the witches, or their demonic superiors, have produced this "vision," to
move Macbeth to do what they want him to do)
47 growing, issuing, springing
48 heat oppressèd = fevered
49 shape
50 (1) perceptible, tangible, (2) plainly observable/apparent
51 guide, usher, lead
52 you are such
53 I was = as I was

Mine eyes are made the fools o'[54] the other senses,
Or else worth[55] all the rest. I see thee still,
And on thy blade and dudgeon[56] gouts[57] of blood,   45
Which was not so before. There's no such thing.[58]
It is the bloody business which informs[59]
Thus to mine eyes. Now o'er the one halfworld[60]
Nature seems dead,[61] and wicked dreams abuse[62]
The curtained sleep.[63] Witchcraft celebrates[64]   50
Pale Hecat's[65] offerings,[66] and withered[67] murder,
Alarumed[68] by his sentinel, the wolf,
Whose howl's his watch,[69] thus[70] with his[71] stealthy pace,[72]
With Tarquin's ravishing strides,[73] towards his design[74]

54 made the fools o' = deceived by
55 worth = are worth
56 hilt
57 drops
58 as you, dagger vision
59 gives shape/form
60 hemisphere
61 (i.e., it is night, and dark: nature "seems" dead because nothing can be seen)
62 misuse, impose upon, cheat, deceive
63 (probably not metaphorical: beds were curtained)
64 ritually solemnizes
65 HEkit (more usually HEkaTEE), goddess of the moon and of sorcery, among other things
66 (i.e., offerings – especially sacrifices – made to the goddess)
67 dried out, arid
68 warned
69 (whose howl is murder's lookout/watchman)
70 accordingly, in accord with his "sentinel" warning(s)
71 (the three iterations of "his" in this and in the preceding line all refer to "murder")
72 step
73 (Tarquin raped Lucretia, who then killed herself: see Shakespeare's narrative poem, *The Rape of Lucrece*)
74 scheme, plan

55   Moves like a ghost. Thou sure[75] and firm set[76] earth,

Hear not my steps, which way they walk, for fear

Thy very stones prate[77] of my whereabout,

And take[78] the present horror[79] from the time,

Which now suits[80] with it. Whiles I threat,[81] he lives:

60   Words to the heat of deeds too cold breath gives.[82]

A BELL RINGS

I go, and it is[83] done. The bell invites[84] me.

Hear it not,[85] Duncan, for it is a knell[86]

That summons thee to[87] heaven, or to hell.

EXIT

75 steadfast

76 firm set = stable

77 chatter, blab

78 acquire

79 present horror = this now and here/actual/immediate horror

80 harmonizes, is fitted/suitable

81 whiles I threat = while/as long as I only threaten (verb)

82 i.e., mere talk breathes too coldly upon the necessarily excited/heated/
passionate nature of actions

83 it is = and then it is/will be done

84 leads/encourages/draws

85 hear it not = do not be aware of/listen to/learn from it

86 slow bell tolling to announce a death or after a funeral★

87 either to

SCENE 2
Macbeth's castle

ENTER LADY MACBETH

Lady Macbeth That which hath made them[1] drunk hath made
   me bold.
   What hath quenched[2] them hath given me fire. Hark, peace.
   (*she listens*) It was the owl that shrieked,[3] the fatal bellman,[4]
   Which gives the stern'st[5] good night. He[6] is about it.[7]
   The doors are open, and the surfeited grooms[8]   5
   Do mock[9] their charge[10] with snores. I have drugged their
   possets,[11]
   That[12] death and nature[13] do contend about them,[14]
   Whether they live or die.
Macbeth   (*within*) Who's there? What, ho![15]
Lady Macbeth Alack,[16] I am afraid they have awaked

---

 1 Duncan's bedroom servants/chamberlains
 2 extinguished, stifled, put an end to (used of fire/flame)
 3 cried, called out (Chaucer said the owl is a prophet "of wo and of
    myschaunce" [misfortune])
 4 town crier (calling and ringing out time, and news, and also bidding good
    nights to all)
 5 most rigorous/severe/inflexible/grim
 6 Macbeth
 7 about it = bringing it to pass, accomplishing it
 8 male servants filled with an excess (of alcohol)
 9 ridicule, flout, set at naught
10 responsibility, duty, trust
11 bedtime drinks: hot milk, alcoholic beverage, sugar, spice, etc.
12 so that
13 the life force
14 about them = over the drunken servants
15 exclamation of excitement, call for attention
16 alas

10   And 'tis not done. The attempt and not the deed
           Confounds[17] us. Hark.[18] I laid their daggers ready,[19]
           He could not miss 'em. Had he[20] not resembled
           My father as he slept, I had done 't.[21]

ENTER MACBETH

                                   My husband?

Macbeth   I have done the deed. Didst thou not hear a noise?

15 *Lady Macbeth* I heard the owl scream and the crickets cry.[22]
           Did not you speak?

Macbeth   When?

Lady Macbeth   Now.

Macbeth   As I descended?[23]

Lady Macbeth Ay.

Macbeth   Hark. Who lies i' the second chamber?

Lady Macbeth   Donalbain.

Macbeth   This[24] is a sorry sight.[25]

20 *Lady Macbeth* A foolish thought, to say a sorry sight.

Macbeth   There's one[26] did laugh in's sleep, and one cried
          "Murder,"

17 defeats, ruins, destroys
18 listen
19 properly arranged
20 Duncan
21 done it myself
22 (both the call of the owl and the chirping of crickets are soft sounds: i.e., the night is quiet)
23 came down (stairs/steps)
24 ("this" seems to refer to what Macbeth has just been seeing, rather than to anything he and his wife now see)
25 sorry sight = weary/dismal spectacle
26 (of the servants)

That[27] they did wake each other. I stood and heard them.
But they did say their prayers, and addressed them[28]
Again to sleep.

Lady Macbeth   There are two lodged[29] together.

Macbeth   One cried "God bless us," and "Amen" the other,   25
As[30] they had seen me with these hangman's[31] hands.
Listening[32] their fear, I could not say "Amen"
When they did say "God bless us."

Lady Macbeth   Consider it not[33] so
deeply.

Macbeth   But wherefore[34] could not I pronounce[35]
"Amen"?
I had most[36] need of blessing, and "Amen"   30
Stuck in my throat.

Lady Macbeth   These deeds must not be thought
After[37] these ways. So,[38] it will make us mad.

Macbeth   Methought[39] I heard a voice cry "Sleep no more,
Macbeth does murder sleep" – the innocent sleep,
Sleep that knits up the raveled sleeve[40] of care,   35

27 so that
28 addressed them = readied/prepared/arranged themselves
29 laid to rest
30 as if
31 executioner's
32 listening to
33 consider it not = don't examine/inspect/scrutinize/think about it
34 why★
35 utter, declare, say
36 very great
37 according to, in the manner of
38 to proceed in this way
39 it seemed to me★
40 frayed/ragged/tangled (1) coarse silk fabric, (2) separate garment worn with
   shirts, etc.

The death of each day's life, sore labor's bath,[41]

Balm[42] of hurt[43] minds, great nature's second course,[44]

Chief nourisher in life's feast[45] –

Lady Macbeth   What do you mean?

Macbeth   Still it cried "Sleep no more," to all the house.[46]

40   "Glamis hath murdered sleep, and therefore Cawdor

Shall sleep no more. Macbeth shall sleep no more."

Lady Macbeth Who was it that thus cried? Why, worthy Thane,

You do unbend[47] your noble strength, to think

So brainsickly[48] of things. Go get some water,

45   And wash this filthy witness[49] from your hand.

Why did you bring these daggers from the place?

They must lie there. Go carry them, and smear

The sleepy[50] grooms with blood.

Macbeth   I'll go no more.

I am afraid to think what I have done.

Look on't again I dare not.

50 *Lady Macbeth*   Infirm[51] of purpose!

41 sore labor's bath = aching/painful toil/exertion's remedial lotion/washing
42 aromatic, healing ointment
43 injured, damaged
44 "second course," grammatically in apposition to (and therefore meaning the
    same as) "chief nourisher," is explained by a historian of table manners as
    follows: "The second course began after all or most of the dishes of the first
    course had been removed from the table ... This consisted of the really big
    pieces ... various roasts, and the spectacular items which the French call
    pièces de résistance" (Margaret Visser, *The Rituals of Dinner* [New York: Grove
    Weidenfeld, 1991], 99)
45 banquet, sumptuous meal★
46 building (the castle)
47 weaken, unstring, undo
48 foolishly, madly, frantically
49 sign, evidence, proof (i.e., blood)
50 somnolent (they are drugged)
51 weak, feeble, frail

Give me the daggers. The sleeping and the dead
Are but as[52] pictures. 'Tis the eye of childhood
That fears a painted[53] devil. If he[54] do bleed,
I'll gild[55] the faces of the grooms withal,
For it[56] must seem their guilt.

EXIT LADY MACBETH
KNOCKING WITHIN

Macbeth   Whence is that knocking?   55
How is't with me, when every noise appals[57] me?
What hands are here? Ha: they pluck out mine eyes.[58]
Will all great Neptune's[59] ocean wash this blood
Clean from my hand? No, this my hand will rather
The multitudinous seas[60] incarnadine,[61]   60
Making the green one[62] red.

ENTER LADY MACBETH

Lady Macbeth My hands are[63] of your color,[64] but I shame[65]

---

52 but as = no more than
53 colored, artificial, pretended
54 Duncan
55 smear
56 (i.e., the blood and therefore the killing which produced it)
57 dismays, weakens, terrifies
58 (*seeing* is conscious, with all the consequences of knowledge, including
responsibility and guilt; *hands* can work more automatically, detached from
consciousness).
59 Neptune = Roman god of the sea
60 multitudinous seas = the immense mass of all the oceans and seas
61 dye red (verb) (i.e., it is more likely that my hand will redden all the
immensity of oceans and seas)
62 (i.e., turning red that which – the ocean – is green)
63 are now
64 (i.e., red with blood)
65 would be shamed (verb)

To wear a heart so white.[66]

KNOCKING WITHIN

              I hear a knocking
At the south entry.[67] Retire we to our chamber.
65 A little water clears[68] us of this deed.
How easy[69] is it then? Your constancy[70]
Hath left you unattended.[71]

KNOCKING WITHIN

              Hark, more knocking.
Get on your nightgown,[72] lest occasion call us,[73]
And show us to be watchers.[74] Be not lost
70 So poorly[75] in your thoughts.
Macbeth To know my deed, 'twere best not[76] know myself.

KNOCKING WITHIN

Wake Duncan with thy knocking: I would[77] thou couldst.

EXEUNT

66 cowardly
67 gate, entrance
68 purifies, frees from guilt (i.e., makes innocent)
69 effortless, simple, comfortable
70 firmness, resolution, fortitude
71 with nothing to serve/wait up on you (i.e., his steadiness has abandoned
    him, like a runaway servant)
72 (a garment not then restricted to female use)
73 occasion call us = circumstances/events summon us/require our presence
74 night watchers, people who stay awake long into the night
75 badly, deficiently, defectively
76 not to
77 wish

SCENE 3
Macbeth's castle

ENTER A PORTER[1]
KNOCKING WITHIN

Porter Here's a knocking indeed! If[2] a man[3] were porter of Hell
gate, he should have old[4] turning the key.

KNOCKING WITHIN

Knock, knock, knock! Who's there, i' the name of
Beelzebub?[5] Here's a farmer, that hanged himself on the
expectation[6] of plenty.[7] Come in time.[8] Have napkins enow[9]   5
about you: here you'll sweat for't.[10]

KNOCKING WITHIN

Knock, knock! Who's there, in the other devil's name?[11]

---

1 gate or door keeper ("janitor")
2 supposing that (i.e., this begins the porter's series of imaginary visitors)
3 (i.e., "any" man, but also "this" man)
4 aged, gotten old (i.e., so busy is *that* gate!)
5 beeELzeBUB: high-ranking devil (i.e., on earth, one says, "In the name of
  God," but in hell, "God" is a nasty word, and one invokes, more properly, one
  of the major devils)
6 on the expectation = in anticipation
7 (i.e., having held back his crops, thinking there would be shortages, the
  farmer commits suicide when he realizes there will be a bountiful harvest
  and his crops will be worth little)
8 come in time = you are / have come in good season (i.e., you belong here)
  (much emended and puzzled over, this brief remark is accurately glossed and
  cited as an illustration by the *OED:* see under the noun "time," entry 46)
9 napkins enow = enough toweling / towels
10 for the double sins of (1) suicide and (2) immoral greed
11 other devil's name = *all* the leading devils' names, according to King James's
  Daemonologie, were really aliases of *the* devil, Satan (*Variorum,* 147, n. to line 10)

Faith,[12] here's an equivocator,[13] that could swear in both the
scales[14] against either scale, who committed treason[15] enough
for God's sake, yet could not equivocate to heaven. O, come
in, equivocator.

KNOCKING WITHIN

Knock, knock, knock! Who's there? Faith, here's an English
tailor[16] come hither, for stealing out[17] of a French hose.[18]
Come in, tailor. Here you may roast[19] your goose.[20]

KNOCKING WITHIN

Knock, knock; never at[21] quiet! What[22] are you? But this
place[23] is too cold for Hell. I'll devil porter it no further: I

12 quasi oath, "by my faith" (deliberately ironic when spoken by a hellish
   porter)
13 one who speaks with deliberate ambiguity (George Sandys [1578–1644]
   wrote in 1599 that "the Jesuits are noted ... to be too hardy [bold, rash]
   equivocators"; and it is the Jesuits in particular who were widely held
   responsible for the Guy Fawkes' or Gunpowder Plot, 1605, intended to kill at
   one blow the king, his ministers, and both houses of Parliament by blowing
   up the building during a royal address to Parliament)
14 one of the two weighing pans in a balance apparatus
15 (to kill the king, God's appointed, was the highest and direst of all capital
   crimes, in addition to being a profoundly ghastly sin)
16 (Wills, *Witches and Jesuits,* 102-3, most persuasively explains the tie between
   this tailor and Father Henry Garnet, a Jesuit executed for complicity in the
   Gunpowder Plot)
17 stealing out = stealing away
18 trousers, leggings
19 (1) heat up, (2) cook (a bird: "cook your own goose" = ruin/kill yourself)
20 an iron used for pressing (so named because the handle resembled a goose's
   neck)
21 staying, remaining
22 what kind of person
23 (castles, made of stone, were notoriously cold)

had thought to have let in some of all[24] professions that go
the primrose way[25] to the everlasting bonfire.

KNOCKING WITHIN

Anon, anon!

OPENS THE GATE

I pray you, remember[26] the porter.   20

ENTER MACDUFF AND LENNOX

Macduff Was it so late, friend, ere you went to bed,
    That you do lie[27] so late?
Porter   'Faith sir, we were carousing[28] till the second cock,[29]
    and drink, sir, is a great provoker[30] of three things.
Macduff What three things does drink especially provoke?   25
Porter   Marry, sir, nose painting,[31] sleep, and urine. Lechery, sir,
    it provokes, and unprovokes. It provokes the desire, but it
    takes away the performance. Therefore, much drink may be
    said to be an equivocator with lechery: It makes him, and it
    mars[32] him; it sets him on,[33] and it takes him off;[34] it   30

24 all the
25 primrose way = pleasant road / path
26 keep in mind, do not forget (i.e., "tip, reward")
27 sleep, lie in bed
28 drinking
29 second cock = the second cock / rooster to crow in the early morning
    (roughly 3 A.M.)
30 inciter, instigator
31 nose painting = red nose due to much drinking
32 stops, hampers, interferes with
33 sets . . . on = (1) builds, erects, puts in place, (2) sharpens, makes keener, (3)
    starts, begins, directs, points, (4) resolves, determines, encourages
34 (1) removes, withdraws, (2) lessens, decreases

persuades him, and disheartens him; makes him stand to,[35]
and not stand to; in conclusion, equivocates him in[36] a sleep,
and, giving him the lie,[37] leaves him.

Macduff I believe drink gave thee the lie last night.

35 *Porter*   That it did, sir, i' the very throat[38] on me. But I
requited[39] him[40] for his lie and, I think, being too strong for
him, though he took up my legs[41] sometime, yet I made a
shift[42] to cast[43] him.

Macduff Is thy master stirring?[44]

ENTER MACBETH

40   Our knocking has awaked him. Here he comes.

Lennox   Good morrow, noble sir.

Macbeth   Good morrow, both.

Macduff Is the king stirring, worthy Thane?

Macbeth   Not yet.

Macduff He did command me to call timely[45] on him.
I have almost slipped[46] the hour.

Macbeth   I'll bring you to him.

---

35 (1) desire, want, hanker for, (2) apply himself, persist, (3) be erect
36 into
37 giving him the lie = deceiving/tricking/betraying him
38 i' the very throat = intensely, foully
39 repaid, retaliated, avenged myself
40 him = it, alcoholic drink
41 took up my legs = (1) made me rise in order to urinate? *or* (2) raised/lifted
my legs, as in wrestling? *or* (3) prevailed?
42 made a shift = managed/found a stratagem/trick/device
43 (1) throw off, defeat, (2) vomit, project (as in urination), (3) defecate
44 moving about ("awake")
45 early
46 missed, neglected

Macduff I know this is a joyful trouble[47] to you,   45
  But yet 'tis one.[48]
Macbeth The labor we delight in physics[49] pain.
  This is the door.
Macduff   I'll make so bold to call,[50]
  For 'tis my limited service.[51]

EXIT MACDUFF

Lennox Goes the king hence today?   50
Macbeth He does. He did appoint[52] so.
Lennox The night has been unruly.[53] Where we lay,
  Our chimneys were blown down and, as[54] they say,
  Lamentings heard i' the air — strange screams of death,
  And prophesying,[55] with accents[56] terrible,   55
  Of dire combustion[57] and confused events
  New hatched[58] to th' woeful time. The obscure bird[59]
  Clamored[60] the livelong night. Some say the earth

---

47 exertion, labor, toil
48 'tis one = it is still a burden ("trouble")
49 alleviates, treats, cures (verb)
50 knock, speak at the door (verb)
51 limited service = appointed/fixed command/responsibility, duty
52 decide, resolve, arrange, fix
53 disorderly, turbulent, stormy
54 so ("according to what")
55 (noun: "lamentings," "screams," and "prophesying" are in parallel/form a series)
56 sounds, tones
57 dire combustion (comBUStion) = horrible/dreadful/evil disorder/tumult/excitement
58 new hatched = newly brought forth/bred
59 obscure bird = dark/gloomy bird (i.e., the owl, prophetic bird of darkness)
60 called loudly

Was feverous[61] and did shake.[62]

Macbeth   'Twas a rough[63] night.

60   Lennox My young remembrance[64] cannot parallel

A fellow to it.

ENTER MACDUFF

Macduff O horror, horror, horror!

Tongue[65] nor heart cannot conceive[66] nor name thee.[67]

Macbeth and Lennox What's the matter?

65   Macduff Confusion[68] now hath made[69] his masterpiece.

Most sacrilegious murder hath broke ope[70]

The Lord's anointed[71] temple, and stole thence[72]

The life[73] o' the building.

Macbeth   What is't you say? The life?

Lennox Mean you his Majesty?

70   Macduff Approach[74] the chamber, and destroy your sight

With a new Gorgon.[75] Do not bid me speak.

See, and then speak yourselves.

61 feverish
62 (a human being "shakes" with fever; the earth "shakes" when experiencing an earthquake)
63 stormy, harsh, violent
64 memory
65 tongue nor heart = neither tongue or heart
66 (1) think of, imagine, (2) comprehend, understand
67 (i.e., the horror)
68 destruction, ruin, disorder★
69 produced, fashioned, created
70 open
71 consecrated
72 from there (i.e., the "temple," meaning the king)★
73 life, spirit, animating principle
74 draw near
75 monster the sight of which turns humans to stone (Medusa was a Gorgon)

EXEUNT MACBETH AND LENNOX

                      (*loudly*) Awake, awake!

Ring the alarum bell. Murder and treason!

Banquo and Donalbain! Malcolm! Awake!

Shake off this downy[76] sleep, death's counterfeit,   75

And look on death itself! Up, up, and see

The great doom's[77] image![78] Malcolm! Banquo!

As from your graves rise up, and walk like sprites,[79]

To countenance[80] this horror! Ring the bell!

BELL RINGS

ENTER LADY MACBETH

Lady Macbeth What's the business,   80

That such a hideous trumpet[81] calls to parley[82]

The sleepers of the house? Speak, speak.

Macduff   O gentle[83] lady,

'Tis not[84] for you to hear what I can speak.[85]

The repetition, in a woman's ear,

Would murder as it fell.[86]

ENTER BANQUO

76 feathery, fluffy
77 judgment of destiny, the Day of Judgment (i.e., universal death)
78 imitation, likeness
79 spirits★
80 face, confirm
81 (here, any powerfully sounding instrument/device)
82 conference, public discussion
83 noble, high ranking★
84 not appropriate/fitting/suitable
85 can speak = am able to say
86 dropped, descended (i.e., was heard)

85   O Banquo, Banquo,
      Our royal master's murdered!
      Lady Macbeth   Woe, alas.
      What, in our house?
      Banquo   Too cruel[87] anywhere.
      Dear Duff, I prithee, contradict thyself,
      And say it is not so.

      ENTER MACBETH AND LENNOX, WITH ROSS

90   *Macbeth*   Had I but died an hour before this chance,[88]
      I had[89] lived a blessèd time, for from this instant
      There's nothing serious[90] in mortality.[91]
      All is but toys:[92] renown and grace[93] is dead,
      The wine of life is drawn,[94] and the mere lees[95]
95   Is left this vault[96] to brag of.

      ENTER MALCOLM AND DONALBAIN

      Donalbain   What is amiss?[97]
      Macbeth   You are, and do not know't.

---

87 (1) pitiless, merciless, (2) fierce, savage
88 unfortunate event
89 would have
90 reliable, steady
91 mortal/human existence
92 games, tricks, jokes, foolish fancies/whims
93 renown and grace = fame and honor/reputation
94 extracted, drained/poured out
95 sediment, dregs
96 wine cellar (a less likely sense of the word – less likely for Macbeth to say,
   though at least an allusion readily recognizable to his audience – is "privy,
   outhouse")
97 wrong, out of order

The spring,[98] the head,[99] the fountain[100] of your blood
Is stopped.[101] The very[102] source of it is stopped.[103]

Macduff Your royal father's murdered.

Malcolm   O, by whom?

Lennox Those of his chamber, as it seemed, had done 't.[104]   100
Their hands and faces were all badged[105] with blood.
So were their daggers, which unwiped we found
Upon their pillows. They stared,[106] and were distracted.[107]
No man's life was to be trusted[108] with them.

Macbeth O, yet I do repent me of[109] my fury,   105
That I did kill them.

Macduff   Wherefore did you so?

Macbeth Who can be wise, amazed, temperate,[110] and furious,
Loyal, and neutral, in a moment? No man.
Th' expedition[111] of my violent love
Outrun the pauser, reason.[112] Here lay Duncan,   110

98 source, origin
99 source, origin
100 head spring, source
101 blocked, brought to a close, caused to cease
102 true
103 (Macbeth utters, in just two lines, four nouns that mean the same thing and
    two verbs, of which those nouns are the grammatical subject, that also mean
    the same thing. Can this be accidental? Can it *not* be meaningful?)
104 had done 't = did it
105 marked
106 looked fixedly, unblinking and, implicitly, without truly seeing
107 (1) deranged, mad, insane, (2) disordered, confused, greatly mentally
    disturbed
108 safe, secure
109 repent me of = regret
110 restrained, forbearing, self-controlled
111 speedy motion / readiness
112 the pauser, reason = that which hesitates, (which is) reason / thought

His silver[113] skin laced[114] with his golden[115] blood,
And his gashed stabs looked like a breach[116] in nature[117]
For ruin's wasteful entrance.[118] There[119] the murderers,
Steeped[120] in the colors[121] of their trade, their daggers

115 Unmannerly breeched[122] with gore.[123] Who could refrain,
That had a heart to love, and in that heart
Courage to make 's[124] love known?

Lady Macbeth   (*fainting*) Help me
hence, ho!

Macduff   Look to[125] the lady.

Malcolm   (*aside to Donalbain*) Why do we hold our tongues,
that most[126] may claim

120 This argument[127] for ours?

Donalbain   (*aside to Malcolm*) What should[128] be spoken here,
Where our fate, hid in an auger[129] hole,

---

113 white as silver
114 embroidered, ornamented, marked, streaked
115 precious, most excellent
116 fracture, rupture, fissure, gap
117 (metrically uncertain, as is much of the play's verse: and his GASHèd
    STABS looked LIKe a BREACH in NAture? and HIS gashed STABS
    looked LIKE a BREACH in NAture?)
118 for ruin's wasteful entrance = because/on account of injury/destruction's
    profitless/useless/prodigal going in/entering
119 there lay/were
120 soaked, bathed
121 (1) the color red, (2) the nature, (3) the distinctive identification
122 unmannerly breeched = rudely covered/clothed
123 thickened (as opposed to fresh) blood
124 make his
125 take care of
126 chiefly, to the greatest extent, best
127 theme, subject matter
128 ought to
129 carpenter's hand tool, for drilling holes

May rush,[130] and seize us? Let's[131] away.
Our tears are not[132] yet brewed.[133]

Malcolm (*aside to Donalbain*) Nor our strong sorrow   125
Upon the foot of motion.[134]

Banquo   Look to the lady:

LADY MACBETH IS CARRIED OUT

And when we have our naked frailties hid,[135]
That suffer in exposure,[136] let us meet,
And question[137] this most bloody piece of work,
To know[138] it further. Fears and scruples[139] shake us.   130
In the great hand of God I stand,[140] and thence[141]
Against[142] the undivulged pretence[143] I fight
Of treasonous malice.[144]

Macduff   And so do I.

130 speedily attack/charge
131 let us go
132 are not = have not been
133 properly made
134 i.e., nor has our powerful grief been started/set/carried/put into motion/ action
135 naked frailties hid = unclothed weaknesses/fragilities (of body) put out of sight/concealed/shielded/covered up (i.e., changed from their sleeping garments into their daytime clothing)
136 suffer in exposure = our "naked frailties" are shameful/painful when left uncovered/unsheltered
137 examine
138 understand, find out about, learn
139 doubts, uncertainties
140 remain
141 from that place, there
142 against . . . I fight = I fight . . . against
143 undivulged pretence = unproclaimed/not publicly known/revealed assertion/claim
144 wickedness

All   So all.

Macbeth Let's briefly[145] put on manly readiness,[146]

And meet i' the hall[147] together.

135 *All*   Well contented.[148]

EXEUNT ALL BUT MALCOLM AND DONALBAIN

Malcolm What will you do? Let's not consort[149] with them.

To show an unfelt sorrow is an office[150]

Which the false[151] man does easy.[152]

I'll to[153] England.

Donalbain   To Ireland, I.

140 Our separated fortune[154] shall keep us both the safer.

Where we are,[155] there's daggers in men's smiles.

The near in blood,[156] the nearer bloody.[157]

Malcolm This murderous shaft[158] that's shot

Hath not yet lighted,[159] and our safest way[160]

145 Is to avoid the aim.[161] Therefore, to horse,

145 quickly
146 preparedness (i.e., clothing and weapons)
147 large room in which banquets and other gatherings took place
148 satisfied, pleased (i.e., "agreed")
149 keep company, associate ourselves, join
150 task, employment
151 deceitful, treacherous, faithless
152 easily
153 go to
154 chance, luck
155 i.e., where we are *now*
156 near in blood = the closer in kinship/blood relationship
157 nearer bloody = more likely bloodthirsty/murderous
158 arrow
159 descended, landed (i.e., the murdering has not yet stopped)
160 course of action ("road, path")
161 direction of the shot

And let us not be dainty of [162] leave taking,
But shift away.[163] There's warrant[164] in that theft
Which steals[165] itself, when there's no mercy left.

EXEUNT

162 dainty of = fastidious/particular/scrupulous about
163 shift away = remove, transfer ourselves (i.e., "get away")
164 (1) protection, security, (2) permission, authorization, justification
165 (1) robs, (2) sneak/slips away

SCENE 4

Outside Macbeth's castle

ENTER ROSS AND AN OLD MAN

Old Man Threescore[1] and ten I can remember well,[2]
Within the volume[3] of which time I have seen
Hours dreadful and things strange. But this sore night
Hath trifled[4] former knowings.[5]

Ross   Ah, good father,[6]

5   Thou seest the heavens, as[7] troubled with man's act,[8]
Threaten his[9] bloody stage.[10] By the clock, 'tis day,
And yet dark night strangles the traveling lamp.[11]
Is't night's predominance, or the day's shame,
That darkness does the face of earth entomb,
When living light should kiss[12] it?

10   *Old Man*   'Tis unnatural,[13]
Even like the deed that's done. On Tuesday last,
A falcon, towering[14] in her pride of place,

---

1 score = 20; threescore = 60; threescore and ten = 70
2 (i.e., not that he *is* age 70 but that he is older than that and can recall 70 years)
3 bulk, space
4 mocked, toyed with, made insignificant
5 personal knowledge/understanding/acquaintance/experience
6 old and venerable man
7 as if they are
8 actions, deeds (i.e., "man" is here universal/plural)
9 man's
10 (i.e., the earth)
11 the traveling lamp = the moving/journeying source of light ("sun")
12 salute, caress
13 abnormal, monstrous★
14 rising high, in order to swoop down onto its prey

Was by a mousing[15] owl hawked at[16] and killed.

Ross　　　And Duncan's horses – a thing most strange and
　　　certain[17] –

　　　Beauteous and swift, the minions[18] of their race,　　　　　　　15

　　　Turned wild in nature, broke their stalls, flung[19] out,

　　　Contending[20] 'gainst obedience, as[21] they would make

　　　War with mankind.

Old Man　　　　　　　　'Tis said they eat[22] each other.

Ross　　　They did so, to the amazement of mine eyes

　　　That look'd upon't. Here comes the good Macduff.　　　　　　20

ENTER MACDUFF

　　　How goes the world, sir, now?

Macduff　　　　　　　　　　　Why, see you not?

Ross　　　Is't known who did this more than bloody deed?

Macduff　　　Those that Macbeth hath slain.

Ross　　　　　　　　　　　　　Alas, the day,

　　　What good[23] could they pretend?[24]

Macduff　　　　　　　　　　　They were suborned.[25]

　　　Malcolm and Donalbain, the king's two sons,　　　　　　25

　　　Are stol'n away and fled, which puts upon them

15 mouse hunting
16 hawked at = attacked/pursued/preyed upon in the air
17 definite, trustworthy, reliable
18 darlings, favorites
19 dashed, ran violently, threw themselves
20 struggling, fighting
21 as if
22 ate, devoured, preyed upon (in England "ate" was and still is pronounced
　　"et")
23 profit, gain
24 they pretend = the dead chamberlains claim/assert
25 corrupted, bribed

Suspicion of the deed.

Ross   'Gainst nature still.
Thriftless[26] ambition, that wilt ravin up[27]
Thine own life's means! Then 'tis most like

30   The sovereignty will fall upon Macbeth.

Macduff   He is already named, and gone to Scone[28]
To be invested.[29]

Ross   Where is Duncan's body?

Macduff   Carried to Colmekill,[30]
The sacred storehouse of his predecessors,
And guardian of their bones.

35 *Ross*   Will you[31] to Scone?

Macduff   No, cousin, I'll to Fife.

Ross   Well, I will thither.[32]

Macduff   Well, may you see things well done there. Adieu,
Lest our old robes sit easier than our new!

Ross   (*to Old Man*) Farewell, father.

40 *Old Man*   God's benison[33] go with you, and with those
That would[34] make good of bad, and friends of foes.[35]

EXEUNT

---

26 unfortunate, unsuccessful, useless, worthless
27 wilt ravin up = desires to (1) steal, plunder, (2) devour
28 village in central Scotland, just N of Perth, possessing a great stone upon
   which, until 1651, the newly crowned kings of Scotland ritually seated
   themselves
29 installed (literally, to be ceremoniously "clothed" in kingly robes)
30 on Iona, a tiny island in the Hebrides
31 will you = will you go
32 (i.e., to Scone)
33 blessing
34 wish to
35 friends of foes = effect reconciliation, bring about peace

Act 3

SCENE I

Forres. The palace

ENTER BANQUO

Banquo Thou[1] hast it now, King, Cawdor, Glamis, all,[2]

As the weird women promised, and, I fear,[3]

Thou play'dst most foully[4] for't. Yet it was said

It[5] should not stand in thy posterity,

But that myself should be the root[6] and father   5

Of many kings. If there come truth from them[7] –

As upon thee, Macbeth, their speeches shine[8] –

Why, by the verities[9] on thee made good,

1 Macbeth
2 thou HAST it NOW king CAWdor GLAMis ALL
3 AS the weird WOMen PROmised AND i FEAR
4 playd'st most foully = acted/worked/operated very deceitfully/falsely ("to play" = to fence)
5 the kingship
6 source, origin
7 the witches
8 are favorable, make a great show
9 truths

May they not be my oracles as well,

10 And set me up in hope? But hush, no more.

> SENNET[10] SOUNDED. ENTER MACBETH, AS KING,
> LADY MACBETH, AS QUEEN, LENNOX, ROSS,
> LORDS, LADIES, AND ATTENDANTS

Macbeth   Here's our chief guest.

Lady Macbeth   If he had been forgotten,
It had been as[11] a gap in our great feast,[12]
And all thing[13] unbecoming.

Macbeth   Tonight we hold a solemn[14] supper, sir,
And I'll request your presence.

15 *Banquo*   Let your Highness
Command[15] upon me, to the which my duties
Are with a most indissoluble tie[16]
Forever knit.

Macbeth   Ride[17] you this afternoon?

Banquo   Ay, my good lord.

20 *Macbeth*   We should have else desired your good advice,
Which still[18] hath been both grave and prosperous,[19]

---

10 trumpets signaling a ceremonial entrance ("fanfare")
11 like
12 banquet, festivity, entertainment
13 completely, wholly
14 ceremonious, formal, grand
15 lay your command
16 are WITH a MOST inDISsolUBle TIE
17 will you be traveling
18 always
19 grave and prosperous = respected/serious/important and auspicious/
   propitious/resulting in success

In this day's council,[20] but we'll take[21] tomorrow.
Is't far you ride?

Banquo   As far, my lord, as will fill up[22] the time[23]
'Twixt this[24] and supper. Go not my horse the better,[25]   25
I must become a borrower[26] of the night
For a dark hour or twain.[27]

Macbeth   Fail not our feast.

Banquo   My lord, I will not.

Macbeth   We hear, our bloody cousins are bestowed[28]
In England and in Ireland, not confessing   30
Their cruel parricide, filling their hearers
With strange invention.[29] But of that[30] tomorrow,
When therewithal[31] we shall have cause of state[32]
Craving[33] us jointly. Hie you to horse. Adieu,
Till you return at night.

                              (*pause*) Goes Fleance with you?   35

Banquo   Ay, my good lord. Our time does call upon 's.[34]

---

20 meeting
21 willingly accept/make do with
22 fill up = occupy
23 as FAR my LORD as WILL fill UP the TIME
24 this time (i.e., "now")
25 go not . . . better = unless my horse does not travel faster
26 temporary user
27 two
28 lodged, located, provided with a resting place
29 strange invention = queer/unaccountable fabrication/fiction
30 of that = we'll talk of that
31 in addition, besides
32 cause of state = matters/considerations of high importance/governmental
   policy
33 calling for/requiring of/needing
34 our time does call upon's = the hour when we must be going summons/
   commands us

Macbeth I wish your horses[35] swift and sure of foot,
   And so I do commend[36] you to their backs.
   Farewell.

EXIT BANQUO

40   Let every man be master of his[37] time
      Till seven at night, to make[38] society
      The sweeter welcome.
      We will keep[39] ourself till suppertime alone.
      While then,[40] God be with you!

EXEUNT ALL BUT MACBETH AND A SERVANT

45   Sirrah,[41] a word with you. Attend those men
      Our pleasure?[42]
Servant They are, my lord, without[43] the palace gate.
Macbeth Bring them before us.

EXIT SERVANT

      To be thus[44] is nothing, but to be[45] safely thus.[46]

35 horses may be
36 entrust, commit (said lightly)
37 his own
38 make society = in order to give/create/produce/prepare for companionship
   to be
39 remain, stay
40 while then = meanwhile, until that time
41 form of address used by a superior speaking to an inferior (or by an adult to a
   child)
42 attend those men our pleasure? = are those men waiting for me to decide to
   see them?
43 outside
44 (i.e., the king)
45 but to be = without being
46 to beTHUS is NOThing BUT to be SAFEly THUS

Our fears in[47] Banquo stick[48] deep,   50
And in his royalty of nature[49] reigns[50] that
Which would[51] be feared. 'Tis much he dares,
And, to[52] that dauntless temper[53] of his mind,
He hath a wisdom that doth guide his valor
To act in safety. There is none but he   55
Whose being[54] I do fear and, under[55] him,
My genius is rebuked,[56] as it is said
Mark Antony's was by Caesar. He chid[57] the sisters[58]
When first they put the name of king upon[59] me,
And bade them speak to him, then prophet like   60
They hailed him father to a line of kings.
Upon my head they placed a fruitless[60] crown,
And put a barren scepter[61] in my grip,
Thence to be wrenched with[62] an unlineal[63] hand,
No son of mine succeeding.[64] If 't be so,[65]   65

47 of
48 stab, thrust★
49 royalty of nature = majestic character
50 predominates
51 should
52 in addition to
53 dauntless temper = bold/fearless quality of balance/calm
54 existence
55 in
56 genius is rebuked = spirit/nature is repressed/put to shame
57 he chid = Banquo complained about/found fault with
58 weird sisters
59 on
60 barren, sterile
61 ornamental rod, symbol of authority
62 by, by means of
63 (i.e., not genetically/lineally descended from Macbeth)
64 coming next, taking my place (as king)
65 thus

For Banquo's issue[66] have I filed[67] my mind.
For them the gracious[68] Duncan have I murdered,
Put rancors[69] in the vessel[70] of my peace
Only for them, and mine eternal jewel[71]

70   Given to the common[72] enemy of man,[73]
To make them kings, the seeds[74] of Banquo kings!
Rather than so, come fate, into the list,[75]
And champion[76] me to th' utterance.[77] Who's there?

ENTER Servant, with two Murderers

(*to Servant*) Now go to the door, and stay there till we call.

EXIT Servant

75   Was it not yesterday we spoke together?
Murderer 1 It was, so please your Highness.
Macbeth   Well then, now
Have you considered of[78] my speeches?[79]

---

66 offspring, descendants★
67 defiled, polluted
68 courteous, indulgent
69 hatred
70 (figurative rather than literal – perhaps "nature, character," as used in Paul's
   Epistle to the Romans, 9.21–23, referring to "vessels of wrath" and "vessels of
   mercy")
71 eternal jewel = immortal soul
72 general, universal
73 (i.e., Satan)
74 issue, descendants
75 roll of combatants (to enter/come into the "lists" as a combatant in a
   knightly tournament)
76 champion me = fight with/against me
77 to th' utterance = to the end/the final extremity ("death")
78 considered of = thought about, reflected on
79 words

Know that it was he[80] in the times past[81]
Which held[82] you so under fortune,[83]
Which you thought had been our innocent self.[84]   80
This I made good[85] to you in our last conference,[86]
Passed in probation[87] with you
How you were borne in hand,[88] how crossed,[89]
The instruments,[90] who wrought[91] with them,
And all things else that might   85
To half a soul and to a notion[92] crazed
Say "Thus did Banquo."

Murderer 1   You made it known to us.

Macbeth   I did so, and went further, which is now
Our point[93] of second meeting. Do you find
Your patience so predominant in your nature   90
That you can let this go? Are you so gospeled[94]
To[95] pray for this good man and for his issue,

80 Banquo (who like Macbeth was a high military officer in Duncan's reign: the
    murderers too are former military men)
81 KNOw that IT was HE in the TIMES PAST
82 kept
83 under fortune = to inferior/lower rank (WHICH held YOU so UNder
    FORtune)
84 our innocent self = guiltless me (WHICH you THOUGHT had BEEN our
    INocent SELF)
85 made good = proved, demonstrated
86 conversation
87 passed in probation = proceeded to/conducted an examination/proof
88 borne in hand = led by the hand ("tricked, deceived")
89 thwarted, afflicted
90 agents, tools
91 worked
92 understanding, mind
93 object, purpose
94 are you so gospeled = have you been so thoroughly preached to/converted
95 as to

Whose heavy hand hath bowed you to the grave

And beggared yours[96] forever?

Murderer 1   We are men, my liege.

95 *Macbeth*   Ay, in the catalogue[97] ye go for[98] men,

As hounds[99] and greyhounds,[100] mongrels,[101] spaniels,[102]

curs,[103]

Shoughs,[104] water rugs,[105] and demi[106] wolves, are clept[107]

All by the name of dogs. The valued file[108]

Distinguishes the swift, the slow, the subtle,[109]

100 The housekeeper,[110] the hunter, every one

According to the gift which bounteous nature

Hath in him[111] closed,[112] whereby he does receive[113]

Particular addition,[114] from[115] the bill[116]

That writes[117] them all alike. And so of men.

96 your family
97 register, rolls
98 go for = pass/are counted as
99 dogs used for hunting by scent
100 dogs used for hunting by sight and speed
101 crossbred dogs
102 dogs used for flushing out and retrieving game
103 watch/shepherd dogs
104 lap dogs (perhaps of Icelandic origin) (SHOCKS?)
105 shaggy water dogs
106 half
107 called
108 valued file = catalogue/listing/roll★ that indicates the value of each item
109 delicate, fine, slender
110 watchdog ("house guardian/watch")
111 it (i.e., the dog in question)
112 set
113 does receive = is given/accorded, gets
114 particular addition = unique/individual characteristics
115 in contrast to, as separated from
116 catalogue, list, inventory
117 enters, describes

Now, if you have a station[118] in the file,

Not i' the worst rank of manhood, say 't,[119]

And I will put that business[120] in your bosoms

Whose execution[121] takes your enemy off,[122]

Grapples[123] you to the heart and love of us,

Who wear our health but sickly[124] in his life,[125]

Which[126] in his death were perfect.[127]

Murderer 2   I am one, my liege,

Whom the vile blows and buffets[128] of the world

Have so incensed that I am reckless what

I do to spite the world.

Murderer 1   And I another

So weary with disasters, tugged with[129] fortune,

That I would set[130] my life on any chance,

To mend it, or be rid on 't.

Macbeth   Both of you know Banquo was your enemy.

Both Murderers True, my lord.

Macbeth   So is he mine, and in such bloody distance[131]

That every minute of his being thrusts

118 position, place★
119 say't = test it, put it to the proof
120 that business = such an affair/action/labor
121 whose execution = the doing/accomplishing of which
122 takes off = kills, carries off, removes
123 and attaches/fastens
124 who wear our health but sickly = I who possess/enjoy my well-being/
    safety only weakly/uncomfortably
125 in his life = while he lives
126 (Macbeth's well-being)
127 were perfect = would be whole, fully sound★
128 strokes
129 tugged with = pulled at by
130 place, stake, wager
131 disagreement, quarrel, estrangement

Against my near'st of life.[132] And though I could
With barefaced[133] power sweep him from my sight
And bid my will avouch it,[134] yet I must not,
125   For certain[135] friends that are both his and mine,
Whose loves I may not drop, but wail[136] his fall
Who I myself struck down. And thence it is,
That I to your assistance do make love,[137]
Masking the business from the common[138] eye
For sundry weighty reasons.

130   *Murderer 2*   We shall, my lord,
Perform what you command us.

Murderer 1   Though our lives —

Macbeth \ (*interrupting*) Your spirits shine through you.[139]
Within this hour at most[140]
I will advise[141] you where to plant[142] yourselves,
135   Acquaint[143] you with the perfect spy o' the time,[144]
The moment on't,[145] for't must be done tonight,

132 near'st of life = most intimate part of my life (i.e., his heart)
133 open, undisguised
134 bid my will avouch it = let my wish/pleasure/decision stand/be
    proclaimed as authority/justification for it
135 for certain = because of some/a number of
136 must lament
137 make love = court
138 public, general
139 shine through you = are clearly evident/visible
140 at most = at the longest
141 notify
142 (verb) post, station
143 I will inform
144 spy o' the time = observation point/ambush for the murder time? (a much-
    debated phrase)
145 moment on't = exact instant of it

And something[146] from the palace, always thought[147]
That I require a clearness.[148] And with[149] him –
To leave no rubs nor botches[150] in the work –
Fleance his son, that keeps him company,   140
Whose absence[151] is no less material[152] to me
Than is his father's, must embrace the fate[153]
Of that dark[154] hour. Resolve[155] yourselves apart.[156]
I'll come to you anon.

Both Murderers   We are resolved, my lord.

Macbeth   I'll call upon you straight.[157] Abide within.[158]   145

EXEUNT MURDERERS

It is concluded.[159] Banquo, thy soul's flight,
If it find heaven, must find it out tonight.

EXIT

146 some way/distance
147 it being always kept in mind/remembered
148 a clearness = personal innocence/freedom from involvement
149 along/together with
150 rubs nor botches = difficulties or bungling
151 disappearance
152 important, of consequence
153 embrace the fate = submit to/accept the destruction/death
154 (1) dim, (2) dismal, (3) hidden
155 decide
156 to one side (i.e., out of Macbeth's presence)
157 directly, immediately, without delay★
158 abide within = wait/remain inside the palace
159 settled, determined, ended

SCENE 2
The palace

ENTER LADY MACBETH AND A SERVANT

Lady Macbeth Is Banquo gone from court?
Servant   Ay, madam, but returns again tonight.
Lady Macbeth Say to the king, I would attend[1] his leisure
   For a few words.
Servant   Madam, I will.

EXIT SERVANT

Lady Macbeth   Nought's had, all's spent,[2]
5   Where our desire is got without content.[3]
   'Tis safer to be that which we destroy[4]
   Than by destruction[5] dwell in doubtful[6] joy.

ENTER MACBETH

   How now, my lord? Why do you keep alone,
   Of sorriest fancies[7] your companions making,
10   Using[8] those thoughts which should indeed have died
   With them they think on?[9] Things without all[10] remedy
   Should be without regard.[11] What's done is done.

1 would attend = wish/would like to expect/look forward to
2 used up, exhausted
3 conTENT
4 that which we destroy = he/the one who we do away with/kill
5 by destruction = because/on account of killing
6 dwell in doubtful = remain/linger in uncertain/fearful/apprehensive
7 sorriest fancies = most distressing/dismal notions
8 frequenting, associating with
9 about
10 any
11 attention, consideration

Macbeth   We have scorched[12] the snake, not killed it.
She'll close and be[13] herself, whilst our poor malice[14]
Remains in danger of her former[15] tooth.   15
But let the frame[16] of things disjoint,[17] both the worlds suffer,[18]
Ere we will eat our[19] meal in fear and sleep
In the affliction of these terrible dreams
That shake us[20] nightly. Better be with the dead,
Whom we,[21] to gain our peace,[22] have sent to peace,   20
Than on the torture of the mind to lie
In restless ecstasy.[23] Duncan is in his grave.
After life's fitful[24] fever he sleeps well.
Treason has done his worst: nor[25] steel, nor poison,
Malice domestic, foreign levy, nothing,   25
Can touch him further.

Lady Macbeth   Come on.[26]
Gentle my lord, sleek[27] o'er your rugged[28] looks.
Be bright and jovial among your guests tonight.

12 slashed (with a knife)
13 close and be = hide and become
14 poor malice = unproductive/unwell/scanty wickedness/power
15 original
16 physical nature/order/structure
17 undo, sever, break up
18 both the worlds suffer = the heavens and the earth be afflicted
19 we ... our = I ... my
20 me
21 I
22 gain our peace = satisfy/attain my ambition
23 (1) frenzy, (2) stupor
24 capricious
25 neither
26 come with me
27 (verb) smooth, polish
28 furrowed, frowning

Macbeth   So shall I, love, and so, I pray, be you.

30   Let your remembrance[29] apply to Banquo.

Present him eminence,[30] both with eye and tongue.

Unsafe[31] the while that[32] we must lave[33]

Our honors in these flattering streams

And make our faces vizards[34] to our hearts,

Disguising what they are.

35   *Lady Macbeth*   You must leave this.

Macbeth   O, full of scorpions is my mind, dear wife!

Thou know'st that Banquo, and his Fleance, lives.

Lady Macbeth But in them nature's copy's[35] not eterne.[36]

Macbeth   There's comfort yet, they are assailable.[37]

40   Then be thou jocund.[38] Ere the bat hath flown

His cloistered[39] flight, ere to[40] black Hecat's[41] summons

The shard[42]-borne beetle with his drowsy[43] hums[44]

Hath rung night's yawning peal,[45] there shall be done

---

29 notice, attention

30 present him eminence = offer/greet him special homage/honor

31 we are unsafe? *or* he (Banquo) is unsafe for/to us?

32 the while that = as long as

33 bathe, wash

34 masks

35 (1) lease (from "copyhold"), *or* (2) reproduction of an image, *or* (3) fullness, plenitude

36 eternal

37 open to assault/attack (in law, vulnerability to legal attack)

38 mirthful, cheerful, merry (JOCKind)

39 reclusive

40 in response to

41 HECates (goddess of night before her transformation into a goddess of magic and witchcraft)

42 wing

43 heavy, sluggish, lethargic, soporific★

44 (noun plural)

45 yawning peal = sleepy bell call

A deed of dreadful note.[46]

Lady Macbeth   What's to be done?

Macbeth   Be innocent of the knowledge, dearest chuck,[47]   45
Till thou applaud the deed. Come, seeling[48] night,
Scarf[49] up the tender[50] eye of pitiful[51] day,
And with thy bloody and invisible[52] hand
Cancel and tear to pieces that great bond[53]
Which keeps me pale![54] Light thickens,[55] and the crow   50
Makes wing to th' rooky[56] wood.
Good things of day begin to droop[57] and drowse,
While[58] night's black agents to their preys do rouse.[59]
Thou marvell'st[60] at my words. But hold thee still.
Things bad[61] begun[62] make strong themselves[63] by ill.[64]   55
So, prithee, go with me.

EXEUNT

46 negative quality/features
47 common term of endearment (from sounds made to pet birds?)
48 stitching up the eyes of a young hawk being trained for falconry
49 blindfold, cover, wrap
50 frail, delicate (as in the young)
51 merciful, compassionate (if, as seems likely, Macbeth is speaking of Banquo's
    lease on life) *or* wretched, contemptible (if, as Wills urges, Macbeth is
    speaking of his baptismal covenant)
52 unseen
53 Banquo's link/connection to nature ("life") *or* as per Wills in note 51, above
54 (i.e., with anxiety, fear)
55 turns dark
56 crow like: (1) dark, (2) full of crows
57 decline, sink down
58 when, as
59 rise up, awaken, become active
60 are astonished/surprised
61 "immoral" bad rather than "incompetent" bad (i.e., begun in order to *be* bad,
    not begun badly)
62 at the start, initially
63 (i.e., make themselves strong)
64 wickedness, evil

SCENE 3

An open place near Macbeth's palace

ENTER THREE MURDERERS

Murderer 1 But who did bid thee join with us?

Murderer 3   Macbeth.

Murderer 2 He needs not our mistrust,[1] since he delivers[2]

Our offices[3] and what we have to do

To the direction just.[4]

Murderer 1   (*to Murderer 3*) Then stand[5] with us.

5   The west yet glimmers with some streaks of day.

Now spurs[6] the lated[7] traveller apace[8]

To gain[9] the timely[10] inn, and near approaches

The subject of our watch.[11]

Murderer 3   Hark, I hear horses.

Banquo   (*within*) Give us a light there, ho!

Murderer 2   Then 'tis he.

10   The rest that are within[12] the note[13] of expectation[14]

Already are i' the court.[15]

1 (i.e., it is not necessary that we mistrust this new recruit)
2 speaks of, describes
3 duties, obligations
4 to the direction just = exactly as we have been ordered/directed
5 (verb) position/station yourself ★
6 hurries (i.e., by literally "spurring" his horse)
7 belated, behind time, delayed
8 at a good pace ("quickly")
9 obtain, secure
10 suitable, fitting
11 lookout, surveillance
12 in
13 list
14 expected guests
15 area immediately around the castle and within its walls ("courtyard")

Murderer 1   His horses go about.[16]

Murderer 3 Almost a mile. But he does usually,
    So all men do, from hence to the palace gate
    Make it their walk.[17]

ENTER BANQUO, AND FLEANCE WITH A TORCH

Murderer 2   A light, a light.

Murderer 3   'Tis he.

Murderer 1   Stand[18] to 't.

Banquo   It will be rain tonight.

Murderer 1   (loudly) Let it come down.   15

THEY SET UPON BANQUO

Banquo   O, treachery. Fly,[19] good Fleance, fly, fly, fly!
    Thou mayst revenge.[20] (to Murderer) O slave!

BANQUO DIES. FLEANCE ESCAPES

Murderer 3 Who did strike out the light?

Murderer 1   Was't not the way?[21]

Murderer 3 There's but one down. The son is fled.

Murderer 2 We have lost best half of our affair.[22]   20

Murderer 1 Well, let's away, and say how much is done.

EXEUNT

16 go about = move in a circular direction
17 usual direction
18 fall
19 flee
20 (verb) revenge me
21 right thing to do
22 business (i.e., what we were supposed to do)

SCENE 4

The palace

A BANQUET HAS BEEN PREPARED. ENTER MACBETH,
LADY MACBETH, ROSS, LENNOX, LORDS, AND SERVANTS

Macbeth	You know your own degrees.[1] Sit down.
	At first and last,[2] the[3] hearty welcome.
Lords	Thanks to your Majesty.
Macbeth	Ourself will mingle with society[4]
5		And play[5] the humble host.
	Our hostess keeps her state,[6] but in best time
	We will require[7] her welcome.[8]
Lady Macbeth	Pronounce[9] it for me, sir, to all our friends,
	For my heart speaks they are welcome.

MURDERER I APPEARS AT THE DOOR

10 | *Macbeth* | (*to Lady Macbeth*) See, they encounter[10] thee with their hearts' thanks.

Both sides[11] are even: here I'll sit i' the midst.

Be large[12] in mirth. (*sees Murderer*) Anon we'll drink a measure[13]

The table round.

---

1 rank, status (i.e., "precedence," seating priority)
2 at first and last = from start to finish ("once and for all")
3 a
4 the party/company
5 (1) act, serve, (2) have the pleasure of being
6 keeps her state = remains seated
7 (1) ask for, request, (2) claim, call for
8 greeting, indication of pleasant reception
9 speak, declare
10 address (verb)
11 (i.e., of the table)
12 (1) ample, abundant, (2) indulgent, free, liberated
13 cup, goblet

APPROACHES MURDERER

There's blood upon thy face.

Murderer 1 'Tis Banquo's, then.

Macbeth 'Tis better thee without, than he within.[14]   15
Is he dispatched?[15]

Murderer 1 My lord, his throat is cut. That I did for him.

Macbeth Thou art the best o' the cutthroats,[16] yet he's[17] good
That did the like for Fleance. If thou didst it,
Thou art the nonpareil.[18]   20

Murderer 1 Most royal sir, Fleance is 'scaped.

Macbeth (*aside*) Then comes my fit[19] again.
I had else been perfect,
Whole as the marble,[20] founded[21] as the rock,[22]
As broad and general[23] as the casing[24] air.   25
But now I am cabined, cribbed, confined, bound in
To saucy[25] doubts and fears. (*to Murderer*) But Banquo's safe?[26]

Murderer 1 Ay, my good lord. Safe in a ditch he bides,[27]
With twenty trenchèd[28] gashes on his head,

14 (i.e., Macbeth prefers to see Banquo's blood on his killer rather than in
Banquo)
15 killed, out of the way
16 (a grisly pun)
17 he's also
18 one without equal/peerless
19 sickness, crisis
20 the marble = marble
21 solidly grounded/based
22 the rock = rock
23 broad and general = ample/fully extended/unrestrained and affable
24 enclosing, surrounding
25 presumptuous, wanton
26 taken care of, secure, free of risk
27 remains, stays, waits
28 deeply furrowed

The least[29] a death to nature.[30]

30 *Macbeth*   Thanks for that.
There the grown[31] serpent lies. The worm[32] that's fled
Hath nature[33] that in time will venom breed,
No[34] teeth for the present. Get thee gone. Tomorrow
We'll hear ourselves again.[35]

EXIT MURDERER

Lady Macbeth   My royal lord,
35 You do not give the[36] cheer. The feast is sold[37]
That is not often vouched.[38] While 'tis a-making,[39]
'Tis[40] given with welcome. To feed[41] were best at home.
From thence,[42] the sauce to[43] meat is ceremony.[44]
Meeting[45] were bare without it.

---

29 least of them
30 (1) life, (2) a human being
31 grown up, matured
32 smaller serpent
33 qualities, properties
34 but no
35 (i.e., we'll discuss matters again – though it is not clear whether "we" and
   "ourselves" are used as "I," Macbeth, or "we," Macbeth and the three
   murderers; if the former, the meaning would be "Tomorrow I will talk and
   you will listen")
36 give the = offer
37 like something paid for / bought and sold (i.e., where people attend like
   mercenaries?)
38 attested to, guaranteed, affirmed
39 taking place, running its course
40 it – a feast – must be (i.e., if it is really a feast / banquet)
41 (used, here, to mean simply taking nourishment, not dining / banqueting)
42 from thence = away from home
43 for
44 following prescribed forms of behavior ("good manners")
45 joining / coming together, assembling

Macbeth   Sweet remembrancer![46]

BANQUO'S GHOST ENTERS AND – UNNOTICED BY MACBETH
OR HIS GUESTS – SITS IN MACBETH'S PLACE

Now, good digestion wait on[47] appetite,   40
And health on both!
Lennox   (*to Macbeth*) May't please your Highness
sit.
Macbeth Here had we now our country's honor,[48] roofed,[49]
Were the gracèd[50] person of our Banquo present,[51]
Who may I rather challenge[52] for unkindness[53]
Than pity for mischance.[54]
Ross   His absence, sir,   45
Lays blame upon his promise.[55] Please't your Highness
To grace us with your royal company?[56]
Macbeth The table's full.
Lennox   Here is a place reserved, sir.
Macbeth (*looking*) Where?
Lennox Here, my good lord.

MACBETH SEES BANQUO'S GHOST

46 in Shakespeare's time, and before, a remembrancer was a court official
   charged with assisting the sovereign
47 wait on = (1) await, be ready for, (2) work on
48 dignitaries, men of distinction
49 all under one roof
50 (1) excellent, gracious, (2) fortunate
51 (i.e., *if* the gracèd person of Banquo *were* present)
52 accuse, call to account
53 lack of consideration, ingratitude
54 some misfortune/accident
55 promise to attend
56 (i.e., sit with us at table)

50   What is't that moves[57] your
      Highness?

Macbeth   Which of you have done this?

Lords   What, my good
      lord?

Macbeth   (*to.Ghost*) Thou canst not say I did it. Never shake
      Thy gory locks at me.

Ross   Gentlemen, rise. His Highness is not well.

55 *Lady Macbeth*   Sit, worthy friends. My lord is often thus,
      And hath been from his youth. Pray you, keep seat.
      The fit is momentary. Upon a thought[58]
      He will again be well. If much you note[59] him,
      You shall offend him and extend his passion.[60]

60   Feed, and regard him not. (*aside to Macbeth*) Are you a man?

Macbeth   Ay, and a bold one, that dare look on that
      Which might appal[61] the devil.

Lady Macbeth   O proper stuff![62]
      This is the very painting[63] of your fear.
      This is the air drawn[64] dagger which, you said,

65   Led you to Duncan. O, these flaws and starts,[65]
      Impostors to[66] true fear, would well become
      A woman's story[67] at a winter's fire,

57 disturbs, excites
58 upon a thought = in an instant
59 notice, pay attention to
60 extend his passion = prolong his attack/fit
61 make pale, dismay, terrify
62 proper stuff = complete/perfect rubbish/nonsense
63 (1) product, (2) representation
64 air drawn = depicted in/out of air
65 flaws and starts = gusts/bursts/squalls and bounds/leaps (nouns)
66 pretenders ("pretending to be")
67 fictitious/traditional/imaginary tale

Authorized by[68] her grandam.[69] Shame itself!
Why do you make such faces? When all's done,
You look but on a stool.[70]

Macbeth   Prithee, see there!   70
Behold – look – lo, how say you?
Why, what care I? (*to Ghost*) If thou canst nod, speak too.
If charnel houses[71] and our graves must send
Those that we bury back, our monuments[72]
Shall be the maws[73] of kites.[74]   75

BANQUO'S GHOST VANISHES

Lady Macbeth (*aside*) What, quite unmanned in folly?
Macbeth   (*aside*) If I stand here, I saw him.
Lady Macbeth   Fie,[75] for shame.
Macbeth   Blood hath been shed ere now, i' the olden time,
Ere human statute purged the gentle weal.[76]
Ay, and since too, murders have been performed   80
Too terrible for the ear. The times have been
That, when the brains were out, the man would die,
And there[77] an end, but now they[78] rise again,

68 passed down/learned from
69 grandmother
70 chair
71 charnel houses = burial places
72 tombs, sepulchers
73 stomachs, bellies
74 birds of prey, vultures★
75 (exclamation of disgust)
76 statute purged the gentle weal = human laws/decrees cleansed/purified
   ("flushed out") the community/state,★ making it courteous/honorable/
   polite
77 there would be
78 (dead men)

With twenty mortal murders on[79] their crowns,

85   And push us from our stools. This is more strange

Than such a murder is.

Lady Macbeth   My worthy lord,

Your noble friends do lack[80] you.

Macbeth   I do forget.

Do not muse at[81] me, my most worthy friends.

I have a strange infirmity, which is nothing

90   To those that know me. Come, love and health to all.[82]

Then I'll sit down. Give me some wine, fill full.

I drink to the general joy o' the whole table,

And to our dear friend Banquo, whom we miss.

Would he were here.

ENTER BANQUO'S GHOST

To all, and him, we thirst,[83]

And all to all.

95 *Lords*   Our[84] duties, and the pledge.[85]

Macbeth   (*seeing Ghost*) Avaunt,[86] and quit my sight! Let the

earth hide thee!

Thy bones are marrowless, thy blood is cold.

Thou hast no speculation[87] in those eyes

79 mortal murders in = fatal/deadly★ attacks, sufficient to kill, upon
   ("covering")
80 (1) stand in need of, (2) miss
81 muse at = wonder at/be astonished by
82 (i.e., he proposes to make a toast)
83 want to drink
84 to our
85 toast offered by Macbeth
86 be off, go away
87 power of sight

Which thou dost glare with!

Lady Macbeth   Think of this, good peers,
But as a thing of custom.[88] 'Tis no other.   100
Only it spoils[89] the pleasure of the time.

Macbeth   (*to Ghost*) What man dare, I dare.
Approach thou like the rugged[90] Russian bear,
The armed[91] rhinoceros, or the Hyrcan[92] tiger –
Take any shape but that![93] – and my firm nerves   105
Shall never tremble. Or be alive again,
And dare me to the desert with thy sword.
If trembling I inhabit[94] then, protest[95] me
The baby of a girl.[96] Hence, horrible shadow!
Unreal mock'ry, hence!

EXIT GHOST

                              Why, so. Being gone,   110
I am a man again. (*to his guests*) Pray you, sit still.

Lady Macbeth   You have displaced[97] the mirth, broke the good meeting,[98]
With most admired disorder.[99]

88 of custom = ordinary, usual
89 detracts from, takes away
90 shaggy
91 equipped for war
92 Persian
93 (the shape the ghost now has)
94 remain
95 declare, affirm★
96 baby of a girl = a girl baby
97 banished, removed
98 gathering
99 admired disorder = astonishing/startling confusion/irregularity

Macbeth   (to Lady Macbeth) Can such
    things be,
    And overcome[100] us like a summer's cloud,
115   Without our special wonder?[101] You make me strange[102]
    Even to the disposition[103] that I owe,[104]
    When now I think you can behold such sights,
    And keep the natural ruby of your cheeks,
    When mine is blanched[105] with fear.

Ross   What sights, my lord?

120 Lady Macbeth I pray you, speak not. He grows worse and worse.
    Question enrages him. At once,[106] good night.
    Stand not[107] upon the order of your going,
    But go at once.

Lennox   Good night. And better health
    Attend his Majesty.

Lady Macbeth   A kind good night to all.

EXEUNT ALL BUT MACBETH AND LADY MACBETH

125 Macbeth   It[108] will have blood. They say, blood will have
    blood.
    Stones[109] have been known to move and trees[110] to speak.

100 overtake
101 special wonder = extraordinary amazement
102 strange . . . to = feel alien/foreign . . . to
103 temperament
104 own, possess
105 made pale
106 at once = to each and all
107 stand not = do not (1) abide by/wait for, (2) proceed/go, (3) preserve/
    retain
108 the ghost
109 (those placed over buried bodies?)
110 (ghosts or other spirits speaking as if from tress?)

Augures[111] and understood relations[112] have
By magot pies, and choughs, and rooks[113] brought forth[114]
The secret'st man of blood.[115] What is the night?[116]

Lady Macbeth Almost at odds[117] with morning, which is which.   130

Macbeth How say'st thou,[118] that Macduff denies his person[119]
At our great bidding?

Lady Macbeth   Did you send to him, sir?

Macbeth I hear it by the way.[120] But I will send.
There's not a one of them[121] but in his house
I keep a servant fee'd.[122] I will[123] tomorrow,   135
And betimes[124] I will, to the weird sisters.
More shall[125] they speak, for now I am bent[126] to know,
By the worst means,[127] the worst. For mine own good,
All causes[128] shall give way. I am in blood

---

111 divining, reading of omens (by trained professional soothsayers/prophets)
112 understood relations = thoroughly comprehended, agreed upon/assumed connections/correspondences/links
113 magot pies ... choughs ... rooks = magpies ... crows/jackdaws ... black crows (birds that employ, or seem to employ, human speech)
114 brought forth = produced, brought to light
115 secret'st man of blood = most clandestine/hidden/concealed murderer
116 what is the night = what time of night is it
117 in conflict
118 how say'st thou = what do you say
119 denies his person = refuses to appear
120 by the way = in passing, incidentally, by chance
121 (i.e., the lords of Scotland)
122 bribed
123 will go
124 (1) early in the morning, (2) speedily★
125 must
126 determined
127 (i.e., by such devilish folk)
128 motives, considerations

140   Stepped in so far that, should I wade no more,
       Returning[129] were as tedious as go o'er.[130]
       Strange things I have in head, that will to hand,[131]
       Which must be acted ere they may be scanned.[132]
    Lady Macbeth You lack the season[133] of all natures, sleep.
145 *Macbeth*   Come, we'll to sleep. My strange and self abuse
       Is the initiate[134] fear that wants hard use.[135]
       We are yet but young in deed.[136]

                          EXEUNT

129 (to the shore from which he started)
130 go o'er = to cross to the far shore
131 to hand = be made physically palpable
132 tested, analyzed
133 seasoning
134 novice's
135 wants hard use = lacks* hardened/laborious application/usage
136 WE are YET but YOUNG in DEED

SCENE 5
A heath

THUNDER. ENTER THE THREE WITCHES, MEETING HECAT

Witch 1 Why, how now, Hecat?[1] You look angerly.

Hecat   Have I not reason, beldams[2] as you are,

    Saucy[3] and overbold? How did you dare

    To trade and traffic[4] with Macbeth

    In riddles[5] and affairs of death,   5

    And I, the mistress[6] of your charms,[7]

    The close contriver[8] of all harms,[9]

    Was never called to bear my part,[10]

    Or show the glory of our art?

    And, which is worse, all you have done   10

    Hath been but for a wayward son,[11]

    Spiteful[12] and wrathful, who, as others do,

    Loves for his own ends, not for you.

    But make amends[13] now. Get you gone,

    And at the pit of Acheron[14]   15

1 HEcat
2 (1) hags, (2) old women
3 presumptuous
4 trade and traffic = deal and negotiate (negative connotations)
5 enigmas, mysteries
6 woman who controls (parallel to "master" for males)
7 spells, incantations ("magic")
8 close contriver = (1) hidden/secret (2) strict manager
9 evil
10 bear my part = wield/maintain/play my allotted function/role/duty
11 wayward son = self-willed/perverse young male
12 contemptuous
13 reparation, compensation
14 hell (in earlier Greek religion, Acheron was only a river in hell/Hades)

Meet me i' the morning. Thither he
Will come to know his destiny.
Your vessels[15] and your spells provide,
Your charms and every thing beside.
20   I am for[16] the air. This night I'll spend
Unto a dismal and a fatal end.[17]
Great business[18] must be wrought ere noon.[19]
Upon the corner of the moon
There hangs a vaporous drop profound.[20]
25   I'll catch it ere it come to ground,
And that, distilled[21] by magic sleights,[22]
Shall raise[23] such artificial[24] sprites
As by the strength of their illusion[25]
Shall draw him on to his confusion.
30   He shall spurn fate, scorn death, and bear

---

15 utensils
16 heading for
17 dismal and a fatal end = terrible/dark/malign and a fated/ominous goal/
purpose
18 (in what Rabb, *Struggle for Stability,* 116, calls "a witch-ridden society," this
was "great" in ways that were powerfully real to Shakespeare's audience)
19 (not daylight noon but nighttime noon, the position of the moon at
midnight: *OED,* under "noon," noun, 4a and 4b; Flint, *Rise of Magic,* 38, cites
the *virus lunare,* "moon foam," described by Lucan [A.D. 39–65], when the
moon "drops foam upon the plants below"; Thomas, *Religion and Decline of
Magic,* 632, notes that "the astrological choice of times was important ...
for the ritual gathering of magical herbs"; Wills, *Witches and Jesuits,* 55,
emphasizes that "some ingredients of witches' spells not only have to be *used*
at night, but *gathered* by night, in order to have full potency")
20 of great depth
21 concentrated, purified
22 methods, skills, devices
23 create, produce
24 produced by "art" ("manufactured")
25 deception

His hopes 'bove wisdom, grace and fear –
And you all know, security[26]
Is mortals' chiefest enemy.

MUSIC

Hark, I am called. My little spirit,[27] see,
Sits in a foggy[28] cloud, and stays for me.   35

SONG WITHIN: "COME AWAY, COME AWAY," &C. EXIT HECAT

Witch 1 Come, let's make haste; she'll soon[29] be back again.

EXEUNT

26 pledge/document guaranteeing payment of a debt (Wall Street deals in
   stocks and bonds, stocks being ownership shares, bonds being "securities");
   Hecat refers to paying for demonic assistance by selling one's soul (Wills,
   Witches and Jesuits, 74, notes that Shakespeare's "audience knew the price of
   power obtained through diabolic intercession")
27 (i.e., her familiar: see act 1, scene 1)
28 (linked to the last line of act 1, scene 1?)
29 (witches moved at supernatural speeds: William Perkins, writing in 1608, and
   quoted by Chandos, *In God's Name,* 133, explains that they claim to be
   "carried through the air in a moment, from place to place")

SCENE 6
The palace [?]

ENTER LENNOX AND ANOTHER LORD

Lennox My former speeches have but hit your[1] thoughts,
　　　Which can interpret[2] further. Only, I say,
　　　Things have been strangely borne.[3] The gracious Duncan
　　　Was pitied of[4] Macbeth. Marry,[5] he was dead,
5　　And the right valiant Banquo walked[6] too late,
　　　Whom, you may say, if 't please you, Fleance killed,
　　　For Fleance fled. Men must not walk too late.
　　　Who cannot want[7] the thought how monstrous
　　　It was for Malcolm and for Donalbain
10　　To kill their gracious father? Damnèd fact,[8]
　　　How it did grieve Macbeth? Did he not straight
　　　In pious[9] rage the two delinquents tear,[10]
　　　That were the slaves of drink and thralls[11] of sleep?
　　　Was not that nobly done? Ay, and wisely too,
15　　For 'twould have angered any heart alive
　　　To hear the men deny 't. So that[12] I say,

---

1 hit your = struck/met with/reached your own
2 explain
3 conducted (from verb "bear")
4 by
5 (exclamation: "Indeed!")
6 was out walking
7 cannot want = can fail to have
8 damnèd fact = cursed deed/crime
9 (1) faithful, loyal, (2) moral (tinted with connotations of fraud)
10 cut up, rip apart
11 captives, prisoners
12 so that = thus

He has borne all things well. And I do think
That had he Duncan's sons under his key –
As, an't[13] please heaven, he shall not – they should find[14]
What 'twere to kill a father. So should Fleance.   20
But, peace, for from broad[15] words and 'cause he[16] failed[17]
His presence at the tyrant's feast, I hear
Macduff lives in disgrace. Sir, can you tell
Where he bestows[18] himself?

Lord   The son of Duncan,
From whom this tyrant holds[19] the due[20] of birth,   25
Lives in the English court, and is received
Of[21] the most pious Edward[22] with such grace
That the malevolence of fortune nothing
Takes[23] from his high respect.[24] Thither Macduff
Is gone, to pray the holy king,[25] upon his aid[26]   30
To wake[27] Northumberland and warlike Siward,[28]

13 an't (and it) = if it
14 discover
15 emphatic, plain
16 (Macduff)
17 did not make
18 lodges, deposits
19 keeps, withholds
20 legal right
21 by
22 King of England
23 removes, subtracts from
24 regard, reputation, favor
25 (i.e., Edward)
26 upon his aid = in aid of Malcolm
27 wake Northumberland = rouse/stir up/excite the population of
   Northumberland, which occupies the lion's share of the border between
   England and Scotland
28 Earl of Northumberland

That, by the help of these – with Him above

To ratify the work – we may again

Give to our tables meat, sleep to our nights,

35   Free from our feasts and banquets bloody knives,[29]

Do faithful[30] homage and receive free[31] honors,

All which we pine for now. And this report

Hath so exasperate the king that he

Prepares for some attempt[32] of war.

Lennox   Sent he to Macduff?

40 *Lord*   He did. And with[33] an absolute "Sir, not I"

The cloudy[34] messenger turns me[35] his back,

And hums, as who should say[36] "You'll rue[37] the time

That clogs[38] me with this answer."

Lennox   And that well might

Advise him[39] to a caution, to hold what distance[40]

45   His wisdom can provide. Some holy angel

Fly to the court of England and unfold[41]

His[42] message ere he come, that a swift blessing

---

29 free from our feasts and banquets bloody knives = release/deliver our feasts
and banquets from the bloody knives

30 true

31 unrestricted, noble

32 effort, trial

33 and with = and after receiving

34 scowling, sullen

35 "turns me": grammatically reflexive, meaning in current usage "turns"

36 who should say = as if to say

37 regret

38 burdens, loads

39 Macduff

40 (i.e., from Macbeth)

41 disclose, explain, make clear

42 (Macduff's)

May soon return to this our suffering country
Under[43] a hand accursed.[44]

Lord   I'll send my prayers with him.[45]

EXEUNT

43 which is now under
44 (i.e., now accursed by/under Macbeth's hand)
45 with him = by means of that "holy angel"

Act 4

SCENE I

A witches' house,[1] *boiling cauldron set in the middle*

THUNDER. ENTER THE THREE WITCHES

Witch 1 Thrice[2] the brinded[3] cat hath mewed.

Witch 2 Thrice and once the hedge pig[4] whined.

Witch 3 Harpier[5] cries "'Tis time, 'tis time."[6]

Witch 1 Round[7] about the cauldron go.

5   In the poisoned entrails throw.[8]

---

1 The Folio gives no specific setting. Editors have supplied "a house," "a desolate place," "a witches' haunt," etc.
2 "three" is an incantatory number, though its precise significance at this point is not understood
3 tawny brown, with streaks of different color
4 hedge pig = hedgehog, urchin (ugly, nocturnal, solitary, and long associated with fairies and demons)
5 familiar spirit
6 (i.e., to begin making their magic)
7 (i.e., joining hands, they begin a witches' spell-making dance, formed in a circle – which sometimes reverses direction – and concocting their magical brew)
8 in the poisoned entrails throw = throw the poisoned entrails in

Toad, that under[9] cold stone
Days and nights has thirty-one
Sweltered venom sleeping got,[10]
Boil thou first i' the charmèd[11] pot.
All   Double, double toil[12] and trouble.[13]   10
Fire burn, and cauldron bubble.
Witch 2 Fillet[14] of a fenny[15] snake,
In the cauldron boil and bake.
Eye of newt[16] and toe of frog,
Wool[17] of bat and tongue of dog,   15
Adder's fork[18] and blindworm's[19] sting,
Lizard's leg and owlet's wing.
For a charm of powerful trouble,
Like a hell broth boil and bubble.
All   Double, double toil and trouble.   20
Fire burn and cauldron bubble.
Witch 3 Scale[20] of dragon, tooth of wolf,
Witches' mummy,[21] maw and gulf[22]

9 lying under
10 sweltered venom sleeping got = has made/produced poison by exuding it like sweat
11 enchanted, bewitched
12 (1) snare, trap, (2) turmoil
13 (1) injury, harm, (2) pain, worry
14 strip, slice
15 from the fens (i.e., marshes, bogs)
16 small salamander-like, tailed amphibian (in Karel Capek's fascinating science fiction novel, *War with the Newts* [1936], newts are thought to be "devils")
17 any short, soft under-hair
18 forked tongue
19 small reptile then thought to be much like the adder
20 flat, horny skinlike plates
21 dried and embalmed human flesh
22 maw and gulf = belly and that belly's ravening appetite

Of the ravined[23] salt sea shark,

25   Root of hemlock digged i' the dark,[24]

Liver of blaspheming[25] Jew,

Gall[26] of goat, and slips of yew[27]

Silvered[28] in the moon's eclipse,[29]

Nose of Turk and Tartar's lips,

30   Finger of birth-strangled[30] babe

Ditch delivered[31] by a drab.[32]

Make the gruel[33] thick and slab.[34]

Add thereto a tiger's chaudron,[35]

For the ingredients of our cauldron.

35   *All*   Double, double toil and trouble.

Fire burn and cauldron bubble.

Witch 2   Cool it with a baboon's blood,

Then the charm is firm[36] and good.

---

23 stuffed with prey *or* ravenous

24 (see act 3, scene 5, note 19)

25 (Jews, and others not Christian – see "Turk and Tartar," just below – were [1] generally considered impious profaners of the "true religion," and [2] not having been ritually christened, were fully amenable to evil magic)

26 (1) liver bile, (2) pus from an infected sore

27 slips of yew = cuttings/shoots from yew trees (which traditionally grew in churchyards and were thought to be poisonous)

28 (1) coated with silvery stuff (even in eclipse, the moon sheds some light), *or* (emended in some texts) (2) sliced, slivered

29 (see act 3, scene 5, note 19)

30 (i.e., killed by the umbilical cord wound around its neck, in the birth process)

31 ditch delivered = born in a ditch

32 prostitute

33 porridge boiled with chopped meat

34 semi-solid

35 entrails ("chawdron")

36 stable, securely fixed

ENTER HECAT[37]

Hecat   O well done! I commend[38] your pains.

And every one shall share i' the gains.   40

And now about[39] the cauldron sing,

Like elves and fairies in a ring,

Enchanting all that you put[40] in.

MUSIC AND A SONG, "BLACK SPIRITS,"[41] &C. EXIT HECAT

Witch 2 By the pricking[42] of my thumbs,

Something wicked this way comes.   45

Open, locks,

Whoever knocks!

ENTER MACBETH

Macbeth How now, you secret, black, and midnight hags?

What is't you do?

All   A deed without a name.[43]

---

37 the Folio adds, "and the other three witches": probably a printer's addition, not supported by the text

38 praise, extol

39 around about

40 have put

41 (the text of this song is given in Thomas Middleton's *The Witch*, where it is sung by Hecate: "Black spirits and white, red spirits and gray, / Mingle, mingle, mingled, you that mingle may! / Titty, Tiffin, / Keep it stiff in. / Firedrake, Puckey, / Make it lucky. / Liard, Robin, / You must bob in. / Round, around, around, about, about! / All ill come running in, all good keep out!" The song is likely to have been traditional, written neither by Shakespeare nor Middleton; *The Witch*, by all scholarly estimates, dates from the period 1610–16)

42 tingling (i.e., an omen)

43 (not true, of course, but there being power in names, as well as responsibility once something *is* named, the witches vigorously deny a name for what they do)

50   *Macbeth* I conjure[44] you, by that which you profess,[45]

        Howe'er you come to know it, answer me.

        Though you untie the winds and let them fight

        Against the churches[46] – though the yesty[47] waves

        Confound[48] and swallow navigation[49] up –

55   Though bladed corn[50] be lodged[51] and trees blown down –

        Though castles topple on their warders'[52] heads –

        Though palaces and pyramids do slope[53]

        Their heads to their foundations – though the treasure

        Of nature's germens[54] tumble[55] all together,

60   Even till destruction sicken[56] – answer me

        To what I ask you.

    Witch 1   Speak.

    Witch 2   Demand.

    Witch 3   We'll answer.

    Witch 1 Say if thou'dst rather hear it from our mouths,

        Or from our masters?

    Macbeth   Call 'em. Let me see 'em.

    Witch 1 (*dancing and chanting*) Pour in sow's blood, that[57] hath
        eaten

44 (1) call upon, (2) demand by supernatural power
45 (1) believe in and practice, (2) declare belief in, falsely, (3) make your
    profession/business; the last named seems most probable
46 religion, *not* church buildings (?)
47 foaming ("yeasty")
48 demolish, ruin
49 boats and ships
50 bladed corn = sheaves of wheat
51 knocked flat
52 guards, sentinels, watchmen
53 bend/move down
54 shoots/sprouts/young branches/vines
55 collapse, fall down violently
56 even till destruction sicken = so much so that ruin has had enough/is revolted
57 a sow that

Her nine farrow[58] – grease that's sweaten[59]   65
From the murderer's gibbet,[60] throw[61]
Into the flame.

All   Come, high or low,[62]
Thy self and office deftly[63] show!

THUNDER. FIRST APPARITION RISES:[64] AN ARMED[65] HEAD

Macbeth   Tell me, thou unknown[66] power –
Witch 1   He knows thy
thought.
Hear his speech, but say thou nought.   70
Apparition 1 Macbeth! Macbeth! Macbeth! Beware Macduff.
Beware the Thane of Fife. Dismiss me. Enough.

THE APPARITION DESCENDS

Macbeth   Whate'er thou art, for thy good caution,[67] thanks.
Thou hast harped[68] my fear aright. But one word more –
Witch 1   He will not be commanded. Here's another,   75
More potent[69] than the first.

THUNDER. SECOND APPARITION RISES: A BLOODY CHILD

Apparition 2 Macbeth! Macbeth! Macbeth!

58 piglets (her whole litter)
59 sweated (to make a rhyme with "eaten," pronounced in England ETen?)
60 bar on which the bodies of executed criminals were hung
61 throw it
62 (i.e., no matter what status/rank)
63 nimbly, skillfully
64 (through a trap door, presumably)
65 armored (i.e., a warrior's head – but whose is uncertain)
66 unfamiliar
67 warning
68 (1) given voice to, (2) guessed, (3) focused most intensively upon
69 powerful

Macbeth   Had I three ears, I'd hear thee.

Apparition 2 Be bloody, bold, and resolute. Laugh to scorn

80   The power of man, for none of woman born

        Shall harm Macbeth.

THE APPARITION DESCENDS

Macbeth   Then live, Macduff. What need I fear of thee?

        But yet I'll make assurance double sure,

        And take a bond of[70] fate. Thou[71] shalt not live,

85   That I may tell pale-hearted fear it lies,

        And sleep in spite of thunder.

THUNDER. THIRD APPARITION RISES: A CHILD CROWNED,
WITH A TREE IN HIS HAND

                                        What is this

        That rises like the issue of a king,

        And wears upon his baby brow the round

        And top[72] of sovereignty?

All   Listen, but speak not to't.

90   *Apparition 3* Be lion mettled,[73] proud, and take no care

        Who chafes,[74] who frets,[75] or where conspirers are.

        Macbeth shall never vanquished be, until

        Great Birnam Wood to high Dunsinane Hill

        Shall come against him.

APPARITION DESCENDS

70 bond of = guarantee from
71 Macduff
72 round and top = crown and pinnacle
73 in vigor/spirit/courage
74 rages, gets excited
75 is tormented/irritated/worried

Macbeth   That will never be.
   Who can impress[76] the forest, bid the tree   95
   Unfix his earth-bound root? Sweet bodements,[77] good.
   Rebellion's dead,[78] rise never till the wood
   Of Birnam rise,[79] and[80] our high-placed Macbeth
   Shall live the lease of[81] nature, pay his breath
   To time and mortal custom.[82] Yet my heart   100
   Throbs to know one thing. Tell me, if your art
   Can tell so much: Shall Banquo's issue ever
   Reign in this kingdom?
All   Seek to know no more.
Macbeth I will be[83] satisfied. Deny me this,
   And an eternal curse fall on you! Let me know.   105

THE CAULDRON DESCENDS

Why sinks[84] that cauldron? And what noise[85] is this?

HAUTBOYS PLAY

Witch 1 Show![86]
Witch 2 Show!
Witch 3 Show!

76 force into service
77 predictions, prophecies
78 (i.e., like Banquo's Ghost)
79 out of the ground
80 and then / thus
81 lease of = contract with / issued by
82 ("die in his bed," rather than at some rebel conspirer's hands)
83 will be = want / demand to be
84 descends
85 (1) music, (2) musicians
86 (1) let it be exhibited / displayed (verb), *or* (2) the display / demonstration, exhibit (noun)

110 *All*   Show his eyes,[87] and grieve his heart.[88]

Come like shadows,[89] so depart.[90]

A SHOW OF EIGHT KINGS APPEARS, THE LAST,
BANQUO'S GHOST, WITH A GLASS[91] IN HIS HAND

Macbeth Thou art too like the spirit of Banquo. Down![92]

Thy crown does sear[93] mine eyeballs. And thy hair,

Thou other[94] gold-bound brow, is like the first.

115   A third is like the former. (*to Witches*) Filthy hags,

Why do you show me this? A fourth. Start,[95] eyes!

What, will the line stretch out to the crack of doom?

Another yet! A seventh! I'll[96] see no more.

And yet the eighth appears, who bears a glass

120   Which shows me many more, and some I see

That[97] two-fold balls[98] and treble scepters[99] carry:

Horrible sight. Now, I see, 'tis true,

For the blood-boltered[100] Banquo smiles upon me,

And points at them[101] for his.

87 show his eyes = let Macbeth see for himself
88 grieve his heart = let Macbeth's heart be pained/afflicted
89 phantoms
90 so depart = and leave the same way
91 mirror ("looking glass")
92 descend, disappear
93 burn, wither
94 thou other = you other
95 explode, burst out of your sockets
96 I wish/want to
97 who
98 two-fold balls = double sceptres, representing two coronation ceremonies:
    King James being first crowned (1567, at age one) as James VI of Scotland
    and then (1603) as James I of England
99 one being used in the Scottish ceremony and two in the English
100 blood-boltered = hair clotted/matted with blood
101 the coronation symbols

APPARITIONS VANISH

What, is this so?[102]

Witch 1 Ay, sir, all this is so. But why   125
  Stands Macbeth thus amazedly?[103]
  Come, sisters, cheer we up his sprites,[104]
  And show the best of our delights.
  I'll charm the air to give a sound,
  While you perform your antic round,[105]   130
  That this great king may kindly say,
  Our duties[106] did his welcome pay.

MUSIC. THE WITCHES DANCE AND THEN VANISH

Macbeth Where are they? Gone? Let this pernicious[107] hour
  Stand aye[108] accursèd in the calendar![109]
  Come in, without there!

ENTER LENNOX

Lennox   What's your grace's will?   135
Macbeth Saw you the weyard[110] sisters?
Lennox   No, my lord.
Macbeth Came they not by you?
Lennox   No indeed, my lord.
Macbeth Infected be the air whereon they ride,

102 true
103 bewildered, astonished
104 spirits
105 antic round = fantastic/grotesque circle dance
106 (1) homage, (2) prescribed/required actions
107 ruinous, destructive, evil
108 forever
109 registers, lists, etc.
110 weird

And damned all those that trust them! I did hear
140   The galloping of horse. Who was't came by?
  Lennox   'Tis two or three, my lord, that bring you word
    Macduff is fled to England.
  Macbeth   Fled to England?
  Lennox   Ay, my good lord.
  Macbeth (*aside*) Time, thou anticipatest[111] my dread exploits.
145   The flighty[112] purpose never is o'ertook[113]
    Unless the deed go with it. From this moment
    The very firstlings[114] of my heart shall be
    The firstlings of my hand. And even now,
    To crown my thoughts with acts, be it thought and done.
150   The castle of Macduff I will surprise,[115]
    Seize upon Fife, give to the edge o' the sword
    His wife, his babes, and all unfortunate souls
    That trace[116] him in his line. No boasting like a fool.
    This deed I'll do before this purpose cool.
155   But no more sights.[117] – Where are these gentlemen?
    Come, bring me where they are.

EXEUNT

111 forestall
112 (1) swift, (2) fleeting, transitory
113 accomplished, performed
114 firstborn impulses / thoughts
115 (1) attack unexpectedly, (2) overcome, capture
116 follow, stem from
117 shows, displays

SCENE 2
Fife. Macduff's castle

ENTER LADY MACDUFF, HER SON, AND ROSS

Lady Macduff What had he[1] done, to make him fly the land?
Ross   You must have patience, madam.
Lady Macduff   He had none.
   His flight was madness. When our actions do not,
   Our fears do make us traitors.
Ross   You know not
   Whether it was his wisdom or his fear.   5
Lady Macduff Wisdom? To leave his wife, to leave his babes,
   His mansion and his titles[2] in a place
   From whence himself does fly? He loves us not,
   He wants the natural touch.[3] For the poor wren,
   The most diminitive[4] of birds, will fight,   10
   Her young ones in her nest, against the owl.[5]
   All is the fear and nothing is the love.[6]
   As little is the wisdom, where the flight
   So runs against all reason.
Ross   My dearest coz,[7]
   I pray you, school[8] yourself. But[9] for your husband,   15

---

1 Macduff
2 possessions
3 quality, capacity, feeling
4 diminutive
5 (comparatively large and fearsome, as well as a legendary hunter)
6 (i.e., fear is everything, in this, and love is nothing)
7 cousin (familiar and fond)
8 discipline, control (verb)
9 as

He is noble, wise, judicious, and best knows
The fits[10] o' the season.[11] I dare not speak much further.
But cruel are the times, when we are traitors
And do not know ourselves, when we hold[12] rumor
20 From[13] what we fear, yet know not what we fear,
But float upon a wild and violent sea
Each way and move.[14] I take my leave of you.
Shall not be long but I'll be here again.
Things at the worst will cease, or else climb upward
25 To what they were before. (*to Lady Macduff's son*) My pretty[15] cousin,
Blessing upon you.

Lady Macduff Fathered he is, and yet he's fatherless.

Ross   I am so much a fool, should I stay longer,
It would be my disgrace and your discomfort.[16]
I take my leave at once.

EXIT ROSS

30 *Lady Macduff*   Sirrah, your father's dead.
And what will you do now? How will you live?

Son   As birds do, mother.

Lady Macduff   What, with worms and flies?

Son   With what I get,[17] I mean. And so do they.

10 paroxysms, crises
11 time, period
12 uphold, believe
13 which stems from, because of
14 each way and move = in all directions
15 (1) fine, (2) clever
16 (i.e., because he would weep)
17 obtain, come to have, catch

Lady Macduff Poor bird! Thou'dst never fear the net[18] nor lime,[19]

The pitfall nor the gin.[20]

Son   Why should I, mother?   35

Poor birds they are not set for.[21]

My father is not dead, for all your saying.

Lady Macduff Yes, he is dead. How wilt thou do for a father?

Son   Nay, how will you do for a husband?

Lady Macduff Why, I can buy me twenty at any market.[22]   40

Son   Then you'll buy 'em to sell again.

Lady Macduff Thou speak'st with all thy wit,[23]

And yet, i' faith, with wit enough for thee.

Son   Was my father a traitor, mother?

Lady Macduff Ay, that he was.   45

Son   What is a traitor?

Lady Macduff Why, one that swears[24] and lies.

Son   And be all traitors that do so?

Lady Macduff Everyone that does so is a traitor, and must be hanged.

Son   And must they all be hanged that swear and lie?   50

Lady Macduff Everyone.

Son   Who must hang them?

Lady Macduff Why, the honest men.

18 bird net (compare fish net)
19 a sticky paste made from holly bark, smeared on trees to attract and catch birds
20 pitfall ... gin = trap with a doorlike device for closing when a bird enters ... snare/trap, etc.
21 poor birds they are not set for = they're not set for *poor* birds
22 (in current usage, "shop, store")
23 mind, intelligence
24 gives his oath

Son   Then the liars and swearers are fools, for there are
55   liars and swearers enow[25] to beat the honest men, and hang
        up them.[26]

Lady Macduff Now, God help thee, poor monkey. But how wilt
        thou do for a father?

Son   If he were dead, you'd weep for him. If you would
60   not, it were a good sign that I should quickly have a new
        father.

Lady Macduff Poor prattler,[27] how thou talk'st!

ENTER MESSENGER

Messenger   Bless you, fair dame. I am not to you known,
        Though in[28] your state of honor[29] I am perfect.[30]
65   I doubt[31] some danger does approach you nearly.[32]
        If you will take a homely[33] man's advice,
        Be not found here: hence,[34] with your little ones.
        To fright you thus, methinks, I am too savage.[35]
        To[36] do worse to you were fell[37] cruelty,

25 enough
26 up them = them up
27 chatterer
28 as to
29 state of honor = honorable/gentle status/condition/rank
30 thoroughly informed
31 fear, suspect★
32 shortly, soon
33 simple, common, humble
34 go away
35 ferocious, wild, harsh
36 yet to
37 ruthless, dreadful

Which[38] is too nigh[39] your person.[40] Heaven preserve you,   70
I dare abide no longer.

EXIT

Lady Macduff   Whither should I fly?
   I have done no harm. But I remember now
   I am in this earthly world, where to do harm
   Is often laudable, to do good sometime
   Accounted dangerous folly. Why then, alas,   75
   Do I put up that womanly[41] defense,
   To say I have done no harm?

ENTER MURDERERS

                 What[42] are these faces?[43]
Murderer 1   Where is your husband?
Lady Macduff I hope, in no place so unsanctified[44]
   Where such as thou mayst find him.
Murderer 1   He's a traitor.   80
Son   Thou liest, thou shag eared[45] villain!
Murderer 1   What, you
   egg![46]

STABBING HIM

38 and that
39 close to
40 bodily presence
41 womanish, fearful
42 who
43 (1) people, (2) appearances
44 dishonorable, sinful, immoral
45 hair shagging over the ears
46 contemptible little brat

Young fry[47] of treachery!

Son   He has killed me, mother.

Run away, I pray you!

DIES. EXIT LADY MACDUFF, CRYING "MURDER!" EXEUNT
MURDERERS, FOLLOWING HER

47 offspring

SCENE 3

England. Before the king's palace

ENTER MALCOLM AND MACDUFF

Malcolm Let us seek out some desolate shade, and there
  Weep our sad bosoms empty.

Macduff   Let us rather[1]
  Hold fast the mortal[2] sword, and like good men
  Bestride[3] our downfallen birthdom.[4] Each new morn
  New widows howl, new orphans cry, new sorrows   5
  Strike heaven on the face, that[5] it resounds[6]
  As if it felt with[7] Scotland and yelled out
  Like[8] syllable of dolor.[9]

Malcolm   What I believe I'll wail,[10]
  What know, believe,[11] and what I can redress,[12]
  As I shall find the time to friend,[13] I will.   10
  What you have spoke, it may be so, perchance.
  This tyrant, whose sole name[14] blisters our tongues,
  Was once thought honest. You have loved him well.

1 instead
2 deadly
3 defend, protect, support
4 inheritance, birthright ("native land")
5 so that
6 echoes, rings
7 along with
8 the same
9 suffering, sorrow, pain
10 cry for/over
11 what know, believe = what I know, I'll believe
12 restore, re-establish, mend
13 (verb) befriend
14 sole name = solitary name ("very name")

He hath not touched[15] you yet. I am young, but something
15   You may discern of[16] him through[17] me, and wisdom[18]
        To offer up a weak poor innocent lamb
        T'appease an angry god.

Macduff   I am not treacherous.

Malcolm   But Macbeth is.
        A[19] good and virtuous nature may recoil[20]
20   In an imperial charge.[21] But I shall[22] crave your pardon.
        That which you are my thoughts cannot transpose.[23]
        Angels are bright still, though the brightest fell.
        Though all things foul would[24] wear the brows[25] of grace,
        Yet grace must still look so.[26]

Macduff   I have lost my hopes.[27]

25 *Malcolm* Perchance[28] even there where I did find my doubts.
        Why in that rawness[29] left you wife and child,
        Those precious motives,[30] those strong knots of love,
        Without leave-taking? I pray you,

15 put his hand on, affected, injured
16 discern of = see/perceive about
17 by means of
18 perhaps it is wisdom for you
19 even a
20 degenerate, recede
21 imperial charge = kingly/regal order/command
22 must
23 (1) translate, (2) alter, change
24 (1) might, (2) wish/desire to
25 countenance, facial expressions
26 like itself
27 (of Malcolm)
28 perhaps you lost them
29 (1) bleakness, harshness, (2) unsheltered, unprotected
30 motivations

Let not my jealousies[31] be your dishonors,
But mine own safeties. You may be rightly just,   30
Whatever I shall think.

Macduff   Bleed, bleed, poor country.
Great tyranny, lay[32] thou thy basis sure,[33]
For goodness dare not check[34] thee. Wear[35] thou[36] thy
wrongs,[37]
The title is affeered.[38] Fare thee well, lord.
I would not be the villain that thou think'st   35
For the whole space[39] that's in the tyrant's grasp,
And the rich East to boot.

Malcolm   Be not offended.[40]
I speak not as in absolute[41] fear of you.
I think our country sinks beneath the yoke.
It weeps, it bleeds, and each new day a gash   40
Is added to her wounds. I think withal
There would be hands uplifted in my right,[42]
And here from gracious England[43] have I offer

31 anxieties, vigilance, suspicions
32 lay down, set, build
33 basis sure = safe/secure foundation
34 block, stop, challenge
35 possess, enjoy
36 (again, the "tyranny," Macbeth's rule)
37 wrongdoings
38 title is afeered = right of possession is confirmed/settled
39 area
40 (Malcolm here launches the "equivocator countering" process by which he
   tests Macduff's genuineness)
41 entire, complete
42 justifiable claim (to the throne of Scotland)
43 (i.e., the King of England)

Of goodly thousands.[44] But for all this,

45   When I shall tread upon the tyrant's head,

Or wear it on my sword, yet my poor country

Shall have more vices than it had before,

More suffer and more sundry[45] ways than ever,

By him that shall succeed.[46]

Macduff   What[47] should he be?

50   *Malcolm* It is myself I mean, in whom I know

All the particulars[48] of vice so grafted[49]

That, when they shall be opened,[50] black Macbeth

Will seem as pure as snow, and the poor state[51]

Esteem him as a lamb, being compared

With my confineless harms.[52]

55   *Macduff*   Not in the legions[53]

Of horrid hell can come a devil more damned

In evils to top Macbeth.

Malcolm   I grant him bloody,

Luxurious, avaricious, false, deceitful,

Sudden,[54] malicious, smacking[55] of every sin

60   That has a name. But there's no bottom, none,

---

44 goodly thousands = excellent thousands of fighting men
45 more sundry = in more different/distinct
46 come to the throne in Macbeth's place
47 who
48 parts, elements
49 fixed, implanted, ingrained
50 made open/public
51 (i.e., Scotland)
52 confineless harms = boundless/unlimited evils
53 vast multitudes
54 rash
55 partaking

In my voluptuousness.[56] Your wives, your daughters,
Your matrons and your maids, could not fill up
The cistern[57] of my lust, and my desire
All continent impediments[58] would o'erbear[59]
That did oppose my will. Better Macbeth   65
Than such an one to reign.

Macduff   Boundless intemperance
In nature[60] is a tyranny. It hath been
The untimely[61] emptying of the happy throne
And fall[62] of many kings. But fear not yet
To take upon you what is yours.[63] You may   70
Convey[64] your pleasures in a spacious[65] plenty,
And yet seem cold, the time[66] you may so hoodwink.
We have willing dames[67] enough. There cannot be
That vulture in you, to devour so many
As will to greatness[68] dedicate themselves,   75
Finding it[69] so inclined.

---

56 addiction to sexual pleasures
57 large vessel for storing liquid, especially water
58 continent impediments = restraining/restrictive/chaste hindrances/
  obstructions
59 overwhelm, crush
60 in nature = of character/temperament
61 premature*
62 the fall
63 (i.e., the throne)
64 conduct (verb)/take privately
65 spacious = (1) ample/extensive, (2) prolonged
66 age ("everyone")
67 women
68 (i.e., to great men like the king)
69 greatness (i.e., Malcolm, as king)

Malcolm   With[70] this there grows
          In my most ill-composed affection[71] such
          A stanchless[72] avarice that, were I king,
          I should cut off[73] the nobles for their lands,
80   Desire his jewels and this other's house,
          And my more having[74] would be as a sauce
          To make me hunger more, that I should forge[75]
          Quarrels unjust against the good and loyal,
          Destroying them for wealth.
Macduff   This avarice
85   Sticks deeper, grows with more pernicious root
          Than summer seeming[76] lust, and it hath been
          The sword of our slain kings.[77] Yet do not fear,
          Scotland hath foisons[78] to fill up your will
          Of your mere[79] own. All these are portable,[80]
90   With other graces weighed.
Malcolm But I have none. The king-becoming graces,
          As justice, verity, temperance, stableness,
          Bounty,[81] perseverance, mercy, lowliness,[82]

70 along with
71 ill composed affection = poor settled/adjusted/controlled emotions
72 unquenchable, unstoppable
73 cut off = bring to an untimely end ("kill")
74 more having = having more
75 invent, contrive, pretend
76 summer seeming = summer appearing/looking (i.e., something that, with
    maturity, can diminish or end)
77 sword of our slain kings = weapon of the kings we have had to kill
78 plenty, abundance
79 absolute (i.e., that which the king holds in his own right)
80 endurable, supportable
81 generosity
82 humility, meekness

Devotion,[83] patience, courage, fortitude,[84]
I have no relish[85] of them, but abound   95
In the division[86] of each several crime,[87]
Acting[88] it many ways. Nay, had I power, I should
Pour the sweet milk of concord into hell,
Uproar[89] the universal[90] peace, confound
All unity on earth.
Macduff   O Scotland, Scotland!   100
Malcolm If such a one be fit to govern, speak.
I am as I have spoken.
Macduff   Fit to govern?
No, not to live. O nation miserable,
With an untitled[91] tyrant bloody sceptered,
When shalt thou see thy wholesome[92] days again,   105
Since that the truest[93] issue of thy throne
By his own interdiction[94] stands accursed,
And does blaspheme his breed?[95] Thy royal father
Was a most sainted king. The queen that bore thee,
Oftener upon her knees[96] than on her feet,   110

83 loyalty
84 moral strength
85 (1) trace, tinge, (2) liking
86 variation, component parts
87 several crime = distinct/separate offence/evil act
88 committing, carrying out
89 throw into confusion
90 whole of nature's/the world's
91 one who has no right
92 healthy, disease free
93 most legitimate, lawful
94 authoritative prohibition/declaration
95 parentage, lineage
96 (i.e., in prayer)

Died every day she lived.[97] Fare thee well.
These evils thou repeat'st[98] upon[99] thyself
Have banished me from Scotland. O my breast,
Thy hope ends here.

Malcolm   Macduff, this noble passion,[100]

115 Child of integrity, hath from my soul
Wiped the black scruples, reconciled my thoughts
To thy good truth and honor. Devilish Macbeth
By many of these trains[101] hath sought to win me
Into his power, and modest[102] wisdom plucks[103] me

120 From over-credulous haste. But God above
Deal[104] between thee and me — for even now[105]
I put myself to[106] thy direction, and
Unspeak mine own detraction,[107] here abjure[108]
The taints[109] and blames I laid upon myself,

125 For[110] strangers to my nature. I am yet
Unknown to woman, never was forsworn,[111]
Scarcely have coveted what was mine own,

---

97 (*timor mortis conturbat me,* "fear of death afflicts me," was a basic prayer in medieval Christianity)
98 recite, related
99 about
100 (which Macduff has just displayed)
101 deceits, treacheries, tricks, traps
102 orderly, well conducted
103 pulls, rescues
104 God . . . deal = let God . . . dispose, handle such matters
105 even now = at this time / right now
106 put myself to = place / commit myself to / under
107 defamation, slander
108 renounce, recant, repudiate
109 blemishes, stains, dishonors
110 as
111 sworn falsely, perjured himself

At no time broke my faith, would not betray
The devil to his fellow, and delight
No less in truth than life. My first[112] false speaking   130
Was this upon[113] myself. What I am truly
Is thine and my poor country's to command –
Whither[114] indeed, before thy here[115] approach,
Old Siward, with ten thousand warlike[116] men
Already at a point,[117] was setting forth.   135
Now we'll[118] together, and the chance of goodness[119]
Be like[120] our warranted quarrel![121]

PAUSE

                            Why are you silent?
Macduff Such welcome and unwelcome[122] things at once
   'Tis hard to reconcile.

ENTER A DOCTOR

Malcolm Well, more anon.[123] (*to Doctor*) Comes the king   140
   forth,[124] I pray you?

112 first ever
113 about
114 to which
115 here = current ("right now")
116 skilled
117 at a point = prepared, ready
118 we'll go
119 good fortune
120 equal to the fortunes of
121 warranted quarrel = justified hostile action (i.e., against Macbeth)
122 welcome and unwelcome = agreeable and disagreeable
123 later, after a while (a "misuse," notes the *OED*, "anon," adverb, 5, since
    "anon" is had always meant "at once"; however, the "misuse" had occurred
    gradually, and is recorded as early as 1526; further, it is used, elsewhere, by
    Shakespeare)
124 directly

Doctor   Ay, sir. There are a crew[125] of wretched souls
      That stay his cure. Their malady[126] convinces[127]
      The great assay[128] of art, but at his touch,
      Such sanctity hath heaven given his hand,
      They presently amend.
145 *Malcolm*   I thank you, doctor.

EXIT DOCTOR

Macduff What's the disease he means?
Malcolm   'Tis called the Evil.[129]
      A most miraculous work in this good king,
      Which often, since my here remain[130] in England,
      I have seen him do. How he solicits[131] heaven,
150   Himself best knows. But strangely visited[132] people,
      All swoln and ulcerous, pitiful to the eye,
      The mere[133] despair of surgery,[134] he cures,
      Hanging a golden stamp[135] about their necks,
      Put on with[136] holy prayers. And 'tis spoken[137]

125 large number
126 scrofula (tuberculosis of the lymphatic glands, leading to swollen neck and
    seriously inflamed joints)
127 overcomes, overpowers
128 endeavor
129 (scrofula was known as the King's Evil, since only the touch of a king's hand
    could cure it; King James of England, for whom this play was written,
    thought himself thus endowed)
130 stay
131 entreats, petitions
132 afflicted
133 sheer, pure
134 medicine ("doctors")
135 coin (minted = "stamped")
136 along with
137 'tis spoken = it is said, they say

To the succeeding royalty[138] he leaves   155
The healing benediction.[139] With[140] this strange virtue[141]
He hath a heavenly gift of prophecy,
And sundry blessings[142] hang about his throne
That speak[143] him full of grace.

ENTER ROSS

Macduff   See who comes here.
Malcolm My countryman.[144] But yet I know him not.[145]   160
Macduff (*to Ross*) My ever gentle cousin, welcome hither.
Malcolm I know him now. Good God, betimes remove
    The means[146] that makes us strangers!
Ross   Sir, amen.
Macduff Stands Scotland where it did?
Ross   Alas, poor country,
    Almost afraid to know itself. It cannot   165
    Be called our mother, but our grave, where nothing[147]
    But who knows nothing is once[148] seen to smile,
    Where sighs and groans and shrieks that rend the air
    Are made, not marked,[149] where violent sorrow seems

138 succeeding royalty = kings of his lineage who follow him
139 blessing, divine grace
140 together with
141 miraculous power
142 declarations of divine favor
143 declare
144 (Ross is identified by his costume; we do not know exactly what, at the
    time, this meant)
145 know him not = cannot recognize/identify him
146 intervening force/agency (i.e., Macbeth)
147 no one
148 ever, at any time★
149 but not noticed

170   A modern ecstasy.[150] The dead man's knell
        Is there scarce asked for who, and good men's lives
        Expire before the flowers in their caps,
        Dying or ere[151] they sicken.

Macduff   O, relation[152] too nice,[153]
        And yet too true.

Malcolm   What's the newest grief?

175 *Ross*   That of an hour's age[154] doth hiss the speaker.
        Each minute teems[155] a new one.

Macduff   How does my wife?

Ross   Why, well.

Macduff   And all my children?

Ross   Well too.

Macduff The tyrant has not battered[156] at their peace?

Ross   No, they were well at peace when I did leave 'em.

180 *Macduff* Be not a niggard[157] of your speech. How goes't?

Ross   When I came hither to transport the tidings,
        Which I have heavily[158] borne, there ran a rumor
        Of many worthy fellows that were out,[159]
        Which was to my belief[160] witnessed the rather,[161]

150 modern ecstasy = a commonplace/ordinary/everyday frenzy/trance
151 before, before ever
152 recital, narration
153 detailed, precise
154 (i.e., news an hour old is already stale)
155 produces, gives birth to
156 struck/operated against
157 miser ("stingy")
158 sorrowfully, laboriously
159 in the field, up in arms (in rebellion against Macbeth)
160 confidence
161 witnessed the rather = attested/proved all the sooner/quicker

For that[162] I saw the tyrant's power[163] afoot.   185
Now is the time of help. (*to Malcolm*) Your eye[164] in Scotland
Would create soldiers, make our women fight,
To doff[165] their dire distresses.

Malcolm   Be't their comfort
We are coming thither. Gracious England hath
Lent us good Siward and ten thousand men.   190
An older and a better soldier none
That Christendom gives out.[166]

Ross   Would I could answer
This comfort with the like! But I have words
That would[167] be howled out in the desert air,
Where hearing should not latch[168] them.

Macduff   What concern   195
they?
The general cause? Or is it a fee[169] grief
Due[170] to some single breast?

Ross   No mind that's honest[171]
But[172] in it shares some woe, though the main part
Pertains to you alone.

Macduff   If it be mine,

162 for that = because
163 army
164 attention, supervision ("active presence")
165 be rid of, throw off
166 gives out = reports, utters, proclaims
167 should
168 (1) grasp, comprehend, (2) receive
169 allotted portion of
170 belonging by right
171 honorable, respectable
172 anything else/otherwise than

200   Keep it not from me, quickly let me have it.

    Ross   Let not your ears despise my tongue forever,

    Which shall possess them[173] with the heaviest sound

    That ever yet they heard.

    Macduff   Humh. I guess at it.

    Ross   Your castle is surprised, your wife and babes

205   Savagely slaughtered. To relate the manner[174]

    Were,[175] on the quarry[176] of these murdered deer,

    To add the death of you.

    Malcolm   (*to Macduff*) Merciful heaven!

    What, man! Ne'er pull your hat upon your brows.

    Give sorrow words. The grief that does not speak

210   Whispers[177] the o'erfraught[178] heart and bids it break.

    Macduff My children too?

    Ross   Wife, children, servants, all

    That could be found.

    Macduff   And I must be from[179] thence?

    My wife killed too?

    Ross   I have said.

    Malcolm   Be comforted.

    Let's make us medicines of our great revenge,

215   To cure this deadly grief.

    Macduff He[180] has no children. All my pretty ones?

173 possess them = put them into the possession of/give/inform them
174 (of their death)
175 would be
176 heap/collection (used of deer killed in a hunt)
177 secretly suggests to/communicates with
178 too heavily burdened
179 away from
180 Macbeth? Malcolm?

Did you say all? O hell kite! All?
What, all my pretty chickens and their dam[181]
At one fell swoop?[182]

Malcolm Dispute[183] it like a man.

Macduff   I shall do so.   220

But I must also feel it as a man.
I cannot but remember such[184] things were,
That were most precious to me. Did heaven look on,
And would not take their part? Sinful Macduff,
They were all struck for thee. Naught[185] that I am,   225
Not for their own demerits,[186] but for mine,
Fell slaughter[187] on their souls. Heaven rest them now.

Malcolm Be this the whetstone[188] of your sword. Let grief
Convert to anger. Blunt not the heart, enrage it.

Macduff O, I could play the woman with mine eyes   230
And braggart with my tongue. But gentle heavens,
Cut short all intermission:[189] front to front[190]
Bring thou this fiend of Scotland and myself.
Within my sword's length set him. If he 'scape,
Heaven forgive him too.

Malcolm   This time[191] goes manly.   235

181 mother
182 fell swoop = the fierce/ruthless/savage pouncing, from a height, of a bird
   down onto its prey
183 struggle with
184 that such
185 the nothing
186 sins, offenses
187 fell slaughter = (verb) slaughter fell
188 sharpening stone
189 pause, interruption
190 front to front = face to face
191 pace, rate of movement (i.e., tune, musical "time")

Come, go we to the king. Our power is ready;
Our lack is nothing but our leave.[192] Macbeth
Is ripe for shaking,[193] and the powers above
Put on[194] their instruments.[195] Receive what cheer you may.
240   The night is long that never finds[196] the day.

EXEUNT

192 permission to go (from King Edward of England)
193 harvesting, being cut down
194 put on = clothe themselves in
195 tools ("weapons, armor")
196 comes upon, meets with, obtains

Act 5

SCENE I

Dunsinane. Macbeth's castle

ENTER A DOCTOR AND A GENTLEWOMAN,
LADY MACBETH'S SERVANT

Doctor   I have two nights watched with you, but can
perceive no truth in your report. When was it she last walked?

Gentlewoman Since his Majesty went into the field, I have seen
her rise from her bed, throw her nightgown upon her, unlock
her closet,[1] take forth paper, fold it, write upon't, read it,   5
afterwards seal it, and again return to bed, yet all this while in
a most fast[2] sleep.

Doctor   A great perturbation[3] in nature, to receive at once
the benefit of sleep, and do the effects[4] of watching.[5] In this
slumbery agitation, besides her walking and other actual   10
performances, what, at any time, have you heard her say?

1 cabinet, cupboard
2 deep, sound
3 disturbance, commotion
4 actions
5 wakefulness, being awake

Gentlewoman That, sir, which I will not report after[6] her.

Doctor   You may to me, and 'tis most meet[7] you should.

Gentlewoman Neither to you nor any one, having no witness to
15   confirm my speech.

ENTER LADY MACBETH, WITH A TAPER[8]

Lo you, here she comes. This is her very guise[9] and, upon my
life, fast asleep. Observe her, stand close.

Doctor   How came she by that light?

Gentlewoman Why, it stood by her. She has light by her
20   continually. 'Tis her command.

Doctor   You see, her eyes are open.

Gentlewoman Ay, but their sense is shut.

Doctor   What is it she does now? Look, how she rubs her
        hands.

25 *Gentlewoman* It is an accustomed action with her, to seem thus
        washing her hands. I have known her continue in this a[10]
        quarter of an hour.

Lady Macbeth Yet here's a spot.

Doctor   Hark, she speaks. I will set[11] down what comes
30   from her, to satisfy[12] my remembrance the more strongly.

Lady Macbeth Out, damned spot. Out, I say! – One, two – why
        then, 'tis time to do't. – Hell is murky. – Fie, my lord, fie. A
        soldier, and afeard? What need we fear who knows it, when

6 subsequent to/following upon Lady Macbeth having spoken
7 proper, suitable
8 candle
9 habit, practice, conduct
10 for a
11 write
12 supply, assure

none can call our power to account? – Yet who would have
thought the old man to have had so much blood in him.   35

Doctor   Do you mark that?

Lady Macbeth The Thane of Fife had a wife. Where is she now? –
What, will these hands ne'er be clean? – No more o' that, my
lord, no more o' that. You mar[13] all with this starting.[14]

Doctor   Go to, go to.[15] You have known what you should   40
not.[16]

Gentlewoman She has spoke what she should not, I am sure of
that. Heaven knows what she has known.

Lady Macbeth Here's the smell of the blood, still. All the perfumes
of Arabia will not sweeten this little hand. Oh, oh, oh!   45

Doctor   What a sigh is there. The heart is sorely charged.[17]

Gentlewoman I would not have such a heart in my bosom for the
dignity[18] of the whole body.

Doctor   Well, well, well.

Gentlewoman Pray God it be,[19] sir.   50

Doctor   This disease is beyond my practice.[20] Yet I have
known those which have walked in their sleep who have died
holily in their beds.

Lady Macbeth Wash your hands, put on your nightgown. Look
not so pale. – I tell you yet again, Banquo's buried. He cannot   55
come out on's[21] grave.

13 interfere, ruin, destroy
14 sudden fear/pain
15 (exclamation of disapproval)
16 addressed to himself? to the gentlewoman?
17 burdened*
18 worth, honor
19 be well
20 professional knowledge/experience
21 of his

Doctor   Even so?[22]

Lady Macbeth To bed, to bed. There's knocking at the gate.

60   Come, come, come, come, give me your[23] hand. What's done
        cannot be undone. – To bed, to bed, to bed!

                    EXIT LADY MACBETH

Doctor   Will she go now to bed?

Gentlewoman Directly.

Doctor   Foul whisperings[24] are abroad.[25] Unnatural deeds
        Do breed unnatural troubles. Infected[26] minds
65   To their deaf pillows will discharge[27] their secrets.
        More needs she the divine[28] than the physician.
        God, God forgive us all! Look after her,
        Remove from her the means of all annoyance,[29]
        And still[30] keep eyes upon her. So, good night.
70   My mind she's mated,[31] and amazed[32] my sight.
        I think, but dare not speak.

Gentlewoman   Good night, good doctor.

                    EXEUNT

22 even so = even thus / in that way (i.e., a mild form of "ah ha!")
23 (presumably as spoken to Macbeth)
24 foul whisperings = loathsome / disgusting rumors
25 circulating in the world outside this castle
26 tainted, contaminated
27 unload, disburden, get rid of
28 priest
29 means of all annoyance = instruments capable of injuring her
30 always
31 checkmated
32 bewildered, astounded, terrified

SCENE 2

The country near Dunsinane

DRUM AND COLORS.[1] ENTER MENTEITH, CAITHNESS,
ANGUS, LENNOX, AND SOLDIERS

Menteith   The English power is near, led on by Malcolm,
    His uncle Siward[2] and the good Macduff.
    Revenges burn in them, for their dear causes[3]
    Would to the bleeding and the grim alarm[4]
    Excite the mortified[5] man.[6]

Angus   Near Birnam Wood   5
    Shall we well meet them. That way are they coming.

Caithness   Who knows[7] if Donalbain be with his brother?

Lennox   For certain, sir, he is not. I have a file
    Of all the gentry. There is Siward's son,
    And many unrough[8] youths that even now   10
    Protest their first of manhood.

Menteith   What does the tyrant?

Caithness   Great Dunsinane he strongly fortifies.
    Some say he's mad. Others, that[9] lesser hate him,

---

1 flags
2 (Duncan's wife was in fact the daughter of the Earl of Northumberland;
  Shakespeare has adjusted history)
3 dear causes = harsh/grievous reasons for action
4 grim alarm = fiercely angry/merciless call to arms
5 (1) pained, humiliated, *or* (2) even a dead
6 (in modern English, the first two iterations of "the," in the last line and a half
  of Menteith's speech, would be without meaning, and the third would mean
  "a")
7 who knows? = does anyone know?
8 unbearded ("not having rough chins")
9 who

Do call it valiant fury. But, for certain,

15 He cannot buckle[10] his distempered[11] cause
Within the belt[12] of rule.

Angus   Now does he feel
His secret murders sticking on his hands,
Now minutely revolts upbraid[13] his faith breach.
Those he commands move only in command,[14]

20 Nothing in love.[15] Now does he feel his title
Hang loose about him,[16] like a giant's robe
Upon a dwarfish thief.

Menteith   Who then shall blame
His pestered[17] senses to recoil and start,[18]
When all that is within him does condemn
Itself for being there?

25 *Caithness*   Well, march we on,
To give obedience where 'tis truly owed.
Meet we[19] the med'cine of the sickly weal,
And with him[20] pour we in our country's purge
Each drop of us.

Lennox   Or so much as it needs,

---

10 (metaphorical)
11 disturbed, troubled
12 (metaphorical)
13 minutely revolts upbraid = every minute rebellions reproach/censure
14 in command = when ordered to, on command
15 nothing in love = not at all in affection/regard
16 (not only metaphorical but directly tied to the previously noted metaphors of "buckle" and "belt")
17 plagued, troubled
18 recoil and start = retire/retreat and twitch/jump
19 we come
20 it (i.e., the "medicine")

To dew[21] the sovereign flower and drown the weeds.   30
Make we our march towards Birnam.

EXEUNT MARCHING

21 moisten

SCENE 3
Macbeth's castle

ENTER MACBETH, DOCTOR, AND SERVANTS

Macbeth Bring me no more reports. Let them fly[1] all!

Till Birnam Wood remove to Dunsinane,

I cannot taint[2] with fear. What's the boy Malcolm?

Was he not born of woman? The spirits that know

5   All mortal consequences[3] have pronounced me[4] thus:

"Fear not, Macbeth. No man that's born of woman

Shall e'er have power upon[5] thee." Then fly, false thanes,

And mingle[6] with the English epicures.[7]

The mind I sway[8] by and the heart I bear[9]

10   Shall never sag with doubt nor shake with fear.

ENTER A SERVANT

The devil damn thee black, thou cream[10]-faced loon![11]

Where got'st thou that goose[12] look?

Servant There is ten thousand –

Macbeth   Geese, villain?[13]

1 them fly = Macbeth's supporters/military men flee/run away from him
2 be affected/hurt/impaired
3 events/sequences that are to come
4 pronounced me = declared/proclaimed to me
5 over
6 unite, join
7 sybarites, gluttons ("fancy pants")
8 am influenced/ruled/controlled
9 pronounced like modern "beer": I have discussed some of the dramaturgical uses of rhyme in "Who Heard the Rhymes"
10 white as cream
11 rogue, idler
12 foolish, simpleminded
13 low rustic ("peasant")

Servant   Soldiers, sir.

Macbeth Go prick[14] thy face, and over red[15] thy fear,

    Thou lily-livered boy. What soldiers, patch?[16]   15

    Death of thy soul, those linen cheeks of thine

    Are counselors[17] to fear. What soldiers, whey[18] face?

Servant The English force,[19] so please you.

Macbeth Take thy face hence.

EXIT SERVANT

            (*calling his servant*) Seyton! –

            (*aside*) I am sick at heart,

    When I behold – Seyton, I say! – (*aside*) This push[20]   20

    Will cheer me ever,[21] or disseat[22] me now.

    I have lived long enough. My way[23] of life

    Is fall'n into the sere,[24] the yellow leaf,[25]

    And that which should accompany old age,

    As[26] honor, love, obedience, troops of friends,   25

    I must not look to have. But, in their stead,

    Curses, not loud but deep, mouth-honor, breath,

    Which the poor[27] heart would fain deny, and dare not.

14 to stick with a pointed instrument
15 over red = redden over, make completely red
16 fool, clown, booby
17 provocation to others
18 watery milk
19 army
20 (1) emergency, (2) attack
21 for all time, forever
22 eject, remove
23 direction, path
24 dry, withered
25 yellow leaf = faded, old
26 like
27 (1) low, inferior, deficient, (2) spiritless, cowardly

Seyton!

ENTER SEYTON

Seyton   What is your gracious[28] pleasure?

30   *Macbeth*   What news more?

Seyton   All is confirmed, my lord, which was reported.

Macbeth I'll fight till from my bones my flesh be hacked.

Give me my armor.

Seyton   'Tis not needed yet.

Macbeth I'll put it on.

35   Send out moe[29] horses, skirr[30] the country round,

Hang those that talk of fear. Give me mine armor.

How does your patient, doctor?

Doctor   Not so sick, my lord,

As she is troubled with thick coming fancies,[31]

That keep her from her rest.

Macbeth   Cure her of that.

40   Canst thou not minister[32] to a mind diseased,

Pluck from the memory a rooted[33] sorrow,

Raze[34] out the written[35] troubles of the brain

And with some sweet oblivious[36] antidote

Cleanse the stuffed[37] bosom of that perilous stuff[38]

---

28 (a formulaic address to those of high station)
29 more ("moe" and "more" still had vaguely different but not always observed
   patterns of usage)
30 search
31 thick coming fancies = swarmingly abundant illusions/hallucinations
32 care for, help
33 deep seated, firmly planted
34 cut, slice
35 preserved, recorded
36 cause of forgetting
37 crammed, filled full
38 CLEANSE the stuffed BOSom OF that PERilous STUFF

Which weighs upon the heart?

Doctor   Therein the patient   45

   Must minister to himself.

Macbeth Throw physic[39] to the dogs, I'll[40] none of it.

   (*to Seyton*) Come, put mine armor on. Give me my staff.[41]

   Seyton, send out − Doctor, the thanes fly from me.

   − (*to Seyton*) Come, sir, dispatch.[42] − If thou couldst, doctor,   50
   cast[43]

   The water[44] of my land, find her[45] disease,

   And purge it to a sound and pristine[46] health,

   I would applaud thee to the very echo,[47]

   That[48] should applaud again. − (*to Seyton*) Pull't off, I say. −

   What rhubarb,[49] cyme,[50] or what purgative drug,   55

   Would scour[51] these English hence?[52] Hear'st thou of
   them?[53]

Doctor   Ay, my good lord. Your royal preparation

   Makes us hear something.

Macbeth (*to Seyton*) Bring it[54] after me.

---

39 medical learning and practice
40 (1) I will have, (2) I want
41 (not a heavy stick, to support him, but slender wood or ivory wand or rod,
   symbolic of commanding office)
42 hurry up
43 inspect
44 urine
45 its
46 fresh
47 to the very echo = so loudly that the applause creates echoes
48 (the echo)
49 (medicinal rather than edible)
50 a kind of flowering herb (pronounced "sime")
51 cleanse, wash
52 away from here
53 (the English)
54 (the armor)

60   I will not be afraid of death and bane,[55]

        Till Birnam Forest come to Dunsinane.

    Doctor (*aside*) Were I from Dunsinane away and clear,[56]

        Profit again should hardly draw[57] me here.

EXEUNT

55 murder
56 free
57 profit again should hardly draw = monetary gain would find it difficult a
second time to attract

SCENE 4

Country near Birnam Wood

DRUM AND COLORS. ENTER, MARCHING, MALCOLM,
SIWARD, AND YOUNG SIWARD, MACDUFF, MENTEITH,
CAITHNESS, ANGUS, LENNOX, ROSS, AND SOLDIERS

Malcolm   Cousins, I hope the days are near at hand

That chambers[1] will be safe.

Menteith   We doubt it nothing.

Siward   What wood is this before us?

Menteith   The Wood of Birnam.

Malcolm   Let every soldier hew[2] him down a bough

And bear't before him. Thereby shall we shadow[3]   5

The numbers of our host[4] and make discovery[5]

Err in report of us.

Soldiers   It shall be done.

Siward   We learn no other but[6] the confident tyrant

Keeps still[7] in Dunsinane, and will endure[8]

Our setting down[9] before 't.

Malcolm   'Tis his main hope.   10

For where there is advantage[10] to be given,[11]

1 the interiors of house ("bedroom" was not at the time the primary meaning
  of "chamber")
2 chop, cut
3 screen, obscure, conceal
4 army
5 reconnaissance, reconnoitering
6 no other but = only that
7 always
8 tolerate, submit to
9 setting down = besieging
10 favorable occasion, opportunity
11 had, gotten

Both more and less[12] have given him the revolt,[13]
And none serve with him but[14] constrainèd things[15]
Whose hearts are absent too.

Macduff   Let our just censures[16]

15   Attend the true event,[17] and put we on[18]
Industrious[19] soldiership.

Siward   The time approaches
That will with due decision[20] make us know
What we shall say we have and what we owe.[21]
Thoughts speculative their unsure[22] hopes relate,[23]

20   But certain issue strokes must arbitrate.[24]
Towards which,[25] advance[26] the war.

EXEUNT, MARCHING

12 more and less = those of higher and of lower rank
13 given him the revolt = revolted/rebelled against him
14 except
15 constrainèd things = forced/compelled persons – depersonalized by being
     called "things" – without will/worth
16 condemnatory judgment/punishment (i.e., of those who have remained
     "loyal" to Macbeth)
17 attend the true event = wait for/take into account what has actually
     happened (i.e., were those who stayed in Macbeth's army "constrained" or
     not)
18 put we on = (1) commit/set/apply ourselves to, (2) hasten to practice
19 skillful, zealous
20 due decision = appropriate/proper/rightful/sufficient finality
21 (1) in fact possess (rather than simply "say" we possess), *or*, less likely, (2) have
     duties/obligations toward
22 doubtful, unreliable, uncertain
23 narrate, report
24 certain issue strokes must arbitrate = a definite/settled outcome must be the
     result of blows/battle
25 ("certain issue")
26 let us proceed with/finish

SCENE 5

Macbeth's castle

ENTER MACBETH, SEYTON, AND SOLDIERS,
WITH DRUM AND COLORS

Macbeth Hang out our banners on the outward walls,
    The cry[1] is still "They come." Our castle's strength
    Will laugh a siege to scorn.[2] Here let them lie
    Till famine and the ague[3] eat them up.
    Were they not forced[4] with those that should be ours,   5
    We might have met them dareful,[5] beard to beard,
    And beat them backward home.

A CRY OF WOMEN WITHIN

                                    What is that noise?
Seyton   It is the cry of women, my good lord.

EXIT SEYTON

Macbeth I have almost forgot the taste of fears.[6]
    The time has been, my senses[7] would have cooled[8]   10
    To hear a night shriek, and my fell[9] of hair
    Would at a dismal treatise[10] rouse and stir

  1 (1) battle cry, (2) shouting
  2 to scorn = in/with mockery/contempt
  3 acute fever (EYgyew)
  4 reinforced, fortified
  5 full of defiance/daring
  6 (I have ALmost forGOT the TASTE of FEARS)
  7 mind, mental faculties
  8 (1) dampened, (2) become cold with fear
  9 shock, head
 10 story, account

As[11] life were in't. I have supped[12] full with horrors.

Direness,[13] familiar to my slaughterous thoughts

Cannot once start[14] me.

ENTER SEYTON

15   Wherefore was that cry?

Seyton   The queen, my lord, is dead.

Macbeth   She should have died hereafter.

There would have been a time for such a word.

Tomorrow, and tomorrow, and tomorrow[15]

20   Creeps in this petty[16] pace from day to day,

To the last syllable[17] of recorded[18] time,[19]

And all our yesterdays have lighted fools

The way to dusty death. Out, out, brief[20] candle.[21]

Life's but a walking shadow,[22] a poor player[23]

25   That[24] struts and frets[25] his hour upon the stage

And then is heard no more. It is a tale

Told by an idiot, full of sound and fury,[26]

Signifying[27] nothing.

11 as if
12 eaten, dined
13 dreadfulness
14 startle
15 (toMORrow AND toMORrow AND to MORrow)
16 petty pace = trivial/insignificant rate of movement
17 bit, trace, hint
18 remembered
19 to the LAST SYLlable OF reCORDed TIME
20 brief candle = quickly burned out ("life")
21 out OUT brief CANdle
22 walking shadow = wandering/vagrant delusive/unreal image/phantom
23 poor player = worthless/insignificant actor
24 who
25 wastes, wears away
26 frenzy, maddened passion/anger
27 meaning

ENTER A MESSENGER

Thou comest to use thy tongue. Thy story quickly!

Messenger Gracious my lord,   30
   I should report that which I say I saw,
   But know not how to do it.

Macbeth   Well, say, sir.

Messenger As I did stand my watch upon the hill,
   I looked toward Birnam, and anon, methought,
   The wood began to move.

Macbeth   Liar and slave!   35

Messenger Let me endure[28] your wrath, if't be not so.
   Within this three mile may you see it coming.
   I say, a moving grove.

Macbeth   If thou speak'st false,
   Upon the next tree shalt thou hang alive,
   Till famine cling[29] thee. If thy speech be sooth,   40
   I care not if thou dost for me as much.
   I pull in resolution,[30] and begin
   To doubt the equivocation[31] of the fiend
   That[32] lies like truth:"Fear not, till Birnam Wood
   Do come to Dunsinane."And now a wood   45
   Comes toward Dunsinane. Arm,[33] arm, and out![34]
   If this which he avouches[35] does appear,

28 suffer
29 famine cling = starvation shrivel/wither
30 pull in resolution = rein in/draw back (1) confidence/certainty, (2)
   determination, steady/unyielding purpose
31 deliberate ambiguity, using words that can mean more than one thing
32 who
33 arm yourselves, prepare for battle (arm ARM and OUT)
34 out of the castle (and into the field of battle)
35 declares, asserts

There is nor[36] flying hence nor tarrying here.

I gin[37] to be aweary of the sun,

50 And wish the estate[38] o' the world were now undone.

Ring the alarum bell! Blow, wind! come, wrack![39]

At least we'll die with harness[40] on our back.

EXEUNT

36 neither
37 start, begin
38 condition, state ("existence")
39 RING the alARum BELL blow WIND come RACK
40 armament, body armor

SCENE 6

Dunsinane. Before the castle

DRUM AND COLORS. ENTER MALCOLM, SIWARD, MACDUFF,
AND THEIR ARMY, HOLDING BOUGHS

Malcolm Now near[1] enough. Your leavy[2] screens throw down
  And show[3] like those you are. (*to Seyward*) You, worthy uncle,
  Shall, with my cousin, your right noble son,
  Lead our first battle.[4] Worthy Macduff and we
  Shall take upon's what else remains to do,   5
  According to our[5] order.
Siward   Fare you well.
  Do we but[6] find the tyrant's power tonight,
  Let us be beaten, if we cannot fight.
Macduff Make all our trumpets speak. Give them all breath,
  Those clamorous[7] harbingers of blood and death.   10

EXEUNT

1 we are near
2 leafy
3 show yourselves
4 battle array, battalion
5 my (the royal "we")
6 do but we = as long as we
7 loud, noisy, urgent

SCENE 7

Macbeth   They have tied me to a stake,[1] I cannot fly,[2]
But, bear-like, I must fight the course.[3] What's he
That[4] was not born of woman? Such a one
Am I to fear, or none.

ENTER YOUNG SIWARD

Young Siward What is thy name?
5   *Macbeth*   Thou'lt be afraid to hear it.
Young Siward No, though thou call'st thyself a hotter[5] name
Than any is in hell.
Macbeth   My name's Macbeth.
Young Siward The devil himself could not pronounce a title[6]
More hateful to mine ear.
Macbeth   No. Nor more fearful.[7]
10 *Young Siward* Thou liest, abhorrèd[8] tyrant. With my sword
I'll prove the lie thou speak'st.

THEY FIGHT. YOUNG SIWARD IS SLAIN

Macbeth   Thou wast born of woman.
But swords I smile at, weapons laugh to scorn,
Brandished by man that's of a woman born.

EXIT. ALARUMS

1 (as in bearbaiting, the bear was tied before the dogs were set on him)
2 (they have TIED me TO a STAKE i CAN not FLY)
3 (1) duration, (2) bearbaiting attacks
4 what's he that = who ("who can there be," the question assuming the answer)
5 angrier, more dangerous
6 name
7 no NOR more FEARful
8 disgusting, detested

ENTER MACDUFF

Macduff   That way the noise is. Tyrant, show thy face!
 If thou be'st slain and with no stroke of mine,   15
 My wife and children's ghosts will haunt me still.[9]
 I cannot strike at wretched kerns, whose arms
 Are hired to bear their staves.[10] Either thou,[11] Macbeth,
 Or else my sword with an unbattered[12] edge
 I sheathe again undeeded.[13] (*indicating direction*) There thou 20
 shouldst be.
 By this great clatter,[14] one[15] of greatest note[16]
 Seems bruited.[17] Let me find him, Fortune,
 And more I beg not.

EXIT. ALARUMS
ENTER MALCOLM AND SIWARD

Siward This way, my lord. The castle's gently rendered.[18]
 The tyrant's people on both sides do fight,[19]   25
 The noble thanes do bravely[20] in the war.
 The day almost itself professes[21] yours,
 And little is to do.[22]

9 forever
10 spear shafts
11 you (will be the man I fight with)
12 not worn/defaced by usage
13 having done/performed nothing
14 quickly repeated clashing noise
15 a person, someone
16 importance, distinction
17 reported
18 gently rendered = quietly handed over/surrendered
19 (i.e., fight on both sides)
20 (1) excellently, (2) valiantly
21 declares, announces
22 is to do = remains to be done

Malcolm   We have met with foes[23]
      That strike beside us.[24]
Siward   Enter, sir, the castle.

EXEUNT. ALARUMS

23 we have MET with FOES
24 strike beside us = fight on our side

SCENE 8
Another part of the battlefield

ENTER MACBETH

Macbeth Why should I play the Roman fool, and die
On mine own sword? Whiles I see lives,[1] the gashes
Do better upon them.

ENTER MACDUFF

Macduff   Turn, hellhound, turn![2]
Macbeth Of all men else[3] I have avoided thee.
But get thee back, my soul is too much charged   5
With blood of thine already.
Macduff   I have no words:
My voice is in my sword, thou bloodier villain
Than terms[4] can give thee out![5]

THEY FIGHT

Macbeth   Thou losest labor.[6]
As easy mayst thou the intrenchant[7] air
With thy keen sword impress[8] as make me bleed.   10
Let fall thy blade on vulnerable crests.[9]

---

1 living men
2 do BETter UPon THEM turn HELL hound TURN
3 all men else = all other men
4 words
5 give thee out = disclose/say you are
6 losest labor = struggle/toil in vain
7 uncuttable
8 mark, affect
9 helmets, heads

I bear[10] a charmèd[11] life, which must not yield[12]
To one of woman born.

Macduff   Despair[13] thy charm,
And let the angel[14] whom thou still[15] hast served
15 Tell thee, Macduff was from his mother's womb
Untimely ripped.

Macbeth Accursèd be that tongue that tells me so,
For it hath cowed[16] my better part of man.[17]
And be these juggling[18] fiends no more believed,
20 That palter[19] with us in a double[20] sense,
That keep[21] the word of promise to[22] our ear
And break[23] it to our hope. I'll not fight with thee.

Macduff Then yield thee, coward,
And live to be the show and gaze[24] o' the time.
25 We'll have thee, as our rarer[25] monsters are,
Painted[26] on a pole, and underwrit,[27]
"Here may you see the tyrant."

10 carry, have
11 enchanted
12 be given/handed over/surrendered
13 give up/cease to hope for
14 Satan (a fallen angel)
15 always
16 intimidated, overawed
17 better part of man = (1) soul? *or* (2) manly courage?
18 cheating, deceiving, trick-playing
19 play fast and loose; deal crookedly/evasively ("equivocate")
20 ambiguous
21 hold, are careful to put/retain
22 for
23 destroy, dissolve, burst, shatter, crush
24 that which is stared at
25 more unusual/exceptional
26 depicted
27 captioned

Macbeth   I will not yield
   To kiss the ground before young Malcolm's feet,
   And to be baited[28] with the rabble's curse.
   Though Birnam Wood be come to Dunsinane,   30
   And thou opposed,[29] being of no woman born,
   Yet I will try the last.[30] Before my body
   I throw[31] my warlike shield. Lay on,[32] Macduff,
   And damned be him that first cries, "Hold, enough!'

EXEUNT, FIGHTING. ALARUMS
RE-ENTER, FIGHTING. MACBETH SLAIN

CALL FOR RETREAT. FLOURISH
ENTER, WITH DRUM AND COLORS, MALCOLM, SIWARD,
ROSS, THE OTHER THANES, AND SOLDIERS

Malcolm I would the friends we miss were safe arrived.   35
Siward   Some must go off.[33] And yet, by these I see,
   So great a day as this is cheaply bought.
Malcolm Macduff is missing, and your noble son.
Ross   Your son, my lord, has paid a soldier's debt.
   He only lived but till[34] he was a man,   40
   The which no sooner had his prowess confirmed
   In the unshrinking[35] station where he fought,
   But like a man he died.

28 tormented
29 opposite me
30 try the last = attempt the last part/conclusion/for the last time
31 place, put
32 lay on = attack/strike vigorously
33 go off = die
34 only lived but till = lived only until
35 firm, unyielding

Siward	Then he is dead?
Ross	Ay, and brought off the field. Your cause of[36] sorrow

45   Must not be measured by his worth, for then

      It hath no end.

Siward   Had he his hurts before?[37]

Ross   Ay, on the front.

Siward   Why then, God's soldier be he.

      Had I as many sons as I have hairs,

      I would not wish them to a fairer[38] death –

      And so, his knell is knolled.[39]

50 *Malcolm*   He's worth more sorrow,

      And that I'll spend for him.

Siward   He's worth no more.

      They say he parted[40] well, and paid his score,[41]

      And so God be with him! Here comes newer[42] comfort.

ENTER MACDUFF, WITH MACBETH'S HEAD

Macduff Hail, King! for so thou art. Behold, where[43] stands

55   The usurper's cursèd head. The time is free.

      I see thee compassed[44] with thy kingdom's pearl,[45]

---

36 cause of = motive for
37 had he his hurts before = were his wounds in front
38 more desirable/reputable
39 rung, sounded
40 departed, died
41 account, reckoning ("debt")
42 different
43 here (on a stick/pole)
44 surrounded
45 finest/most noble men

That[46] speak my salutation[47] in their minds,
Whose voices I desire aloud with mine:
Hail, King of Scotland!

All   Hail, King of Scotland!

FLOURISH

Malcolm We shall not spend a large expense of time[48]   60
Before we reckon with[49] your several[50] loves,[51]
And make us even[52] with you. My thanes and kinsmen,
Henceforth be earls, the first that ever Scotland
In such an honor named. What's more[53] to do,
Which would be planted newly with the time,   65
As calling home our exiled friends abroad
That[54] fled the snares of watchful tyranny;
Producing forth[55] the cruel ministers[56]
Of this dead butcher and his fiend-like queen,
Who, as 'tis thought, by self and violent[57] hands   70
Took off[58] her life — this, and what needful else

46 who
47 salute
48 large expense of time = protracted/long interval
49 enumerate, list
50 distinct, particular, individual
51 affection, devotion
52 balanced ("square")
53 left still
54 who
55 bringing forward/into the open (out of hiding)
56 proDUCing FORTH the CRUel MINisTERS
57 by self and violent = by herself and violent
58 took off = did away with, removed, destroyed

That calls upon[59] us, by the grace of Grace
We will perform in measure,[60] time and place.
So thanks to all at once and to each one,
75 Whom we invite to see us crowned at Scone.[61]

FLOURISH. EXEUNT

59 calls upon = summons, commands
60 proportion, degree
61 (probably rhyming with "one")

AN ESSAY BY HAROLD BLOOM

Theatrical tradition has made *Macbeth* the unluckiest of all Shakespeare's plays, particularly for those who act in it. Macbeth himself can be termed the unluckiest of all Shakespearean protagonists, precisely because he is the most imaginative. A great killing machine, Macbeth is endowed by Shakespeare with something less than ordinary intelligence, but with a power of fantasy so enormous that pragmatically it seems to be Shakespeare's own. No other drama by Shakespeare—not even *King Lear, A Midsummer Night's Dream,* or *The Tempest*—so engulfs us in a phantasmagoria. The magic in *A Midsummer Night's Dream* and *The Tempest* is crucially effectual, while there is no overt magic or witchcraft in *King Lear,* though we sometimes half expect it because the drama is of such hallucinatory intensity.

The witchcraft in *Macbeth,* though pervasive, cannot alter material events, yet hallucination can and does. The rough magic in *Macbeth* is wholly Shakespeare's; he indulges his own imagination as never before, seeking to find its moral limits (if any). I do not suggest that Macbeth represents Shakespeare, in any of the complex ways that Falstaff and Hamlet may represent certain inner aspects of the playwright. But in the Renaissance sense of imagination (which is not ours), Macbeth may well be the emblem of that faculty in Shakespeare, a faculty that must have frightened Shakespeare and ought to terrify us, when we read or attend *Macbeth,* for the play depends upon its horror of its own imaginings. Imagination (or fancy) is an equivocal matter for Shakespeare and his era, where it meant both poetic furor, as a kind of substitute for divine inspiration, and a gap torn in reality, almost a punishment for the displacement of the sacred into the secular. Shakespeare somewhat mitigates the negative aura of fantasy in his other plays, but not in *Macbeth,* which is a tragedy of the imagination. Though the play triumphantly proclaims, "The time is free," when Macbeth is killed, the reverberations we cannot escape as we leave the theater or close the book have little to do with our freedom.

Hamlet dies into freedom, perhaps even augmenting our own liberty, but Macbeth's dying is less of a release for us. The universal reaction to Macbeth is that we identify with him, or at least with his imagination. Richard III, Iago, and Edmund are hero-villains; to call Macbeth one of that company seems all wrong. They delight in their wickedness; Macbeth suffers intensely from knowing that he does evil, and that he must go on doing ever worse. Shakespeare rather dreadfully sees to it that *we are* Macbeth; our identity with him is involuntary but inescapable. All of us possess, to one degree or another, a proleptic imagination; in Macbeth, it is absolute. He scarcely is conscious of an ambition, desire, or wish before he *sees* himself on the other side or shore, already having performed the crime that equivocally fulfills ambition. Macbeth terrifies us partly because that aspect of our own imagination is so frightening: it seems to make us murderers, thieves, usurpers, and rapists.

Why are we unable to resist identifying with Macbeth? He so

dominates his play that we have nowhere else to turn. Lady Macbeth is a powerful character, but Shakespeare gets her off the stage after act 3, scene 4, except for her short return in a state of madness at the start of act 5. Shakespeare had killed off Mercutio early to keep him from stealing *Romeo and Juliet,* and had allowed Falstaff only a reported death scene so as to prevent Sir John from dwarfing the "reformed" Hal in *Henry V.* Once Lady Macbeth has been removed, the only real presence on the stage is Macbeth's. Shrewdly, Shakespeare does little to individualize Duncan, Banquo, Macduff, and Malcolm. The drunken porter, Macduff's little son, and Lady Macduff are more vivid in their brief appearances than are all the secondary males in the play, who are wrapped in a common grayness. Since Macbeth speaks fully a third of the drama's lines, and Lady Macbeth's role is truncated, Shakespeare's design upon us is manifest. We are to journey inward to Macbeth's heart of darkness, and there we will find ourselves more truly and more strange, murderers in and of the spirit.

The terror of this play, most ably discussed by Wilbur Sanders, is deliberate and salutary. If we are compelled to identify with Macbeth, and he appalls us (and himself), then we ourselves must be fearsome also. Working against the Aristotelian formula for tragedy, Shakespeare deluges us with fear and pity, not to purge us but for a sort of purposiveness without purpose that no interpretation wholly comprehends. The sublimity of Macbeth and of Lady Macbeth is overwhelming: they are persuasive and valuable personalities, profoundly in love with each other. Indeed, with surpassing irony Shakespeare presents them as the happiest married couple in all his work. And they are anything but two fiends, despite their dreadful crimes and deserved catastrophes. So rapid and foreshortened is their play (about half the length of *Hamlet*) that we are given no leisure to confront their descent into hell as it happens. Something vital in us is bewildered by the evanescence of their better natures, though Shakespeare gives us emblems enough of the way down and out.

Macbeth is an uncanny unity of setting, plot, and characters, fused together beyond comparison with any other play of Shakespeare's. The drama's cosmos is more drastic and alienated even than *King Lear*'s, where nature was so radically wounded. *King Lear* was pre-Christian, whereas *Macbeth,* overtly medieval Catholic, seems less set in Scotland than in the *kenoma,* the cosmological emptiness of our world as described by the ancient gnostic heretics. Shakespeare knew at least something of gnosticism through the Hermetic philosophy of Giordano Bruno, though I think there can be little or no possibility of a direct influence of Bruno on Shakespeare (despite the interesting surmises of Frances Yates). Yet the gnostic horror of time seems to have infiltrated *Macbeth,* emanating from the not-less-than-universal nature of Shakespeare's own consciousness. The world of *Macbeth* is one into which we *have been thrown,* a dungeon for tyrants and victims alike. If *Lear* was pre-Christian, then *Macbeth* is weirdly post-Christian. There are, as we have seen, Christian intimations that haunt the pagans of *Lear,* though to no purpose or effect. Despite some desperate allusions by several of the characters, *Macbeth* allows no relevance to Christian revelation. Macbeth is the deceitful "man of blood" abhorred by the Psalms and elsewhere in the Bible, but he scarcely can be assimilated to biblical villainy. There is nothing specifically anti-Christian in his crimes; they would offend virtually every vision of the sacred and the moral that human chronicle has known. That may be why Akira Kurosawa's *Throne of Blood* is so uncannily the most successful film version of *Macbeth,* though it departs very far from the specifics of Shakespeare's play. Macbeth's tragedy, like Hamlet's, Lear's, and Othello's, is so universal that a strictly Christian context is inadequate to it.

I have ventured in other publications my surmise that Shakespeare intentionally evades (or even blurs) Christian categories throughout his work. He is anything but a devotional poet and dramatist; there are no *Holy Sonnets* by Shakespeare. Even Sonnet 146 ("Poor soul, the centre of my sinful earth") is an equivocal poem, particularly in its crucial eleventh line: "Buy terms divine in selling hours of dross." One major edition of Shakespeare glosses "terms divine" as "everlasting life," but "terms" allows several less ambitious readings. Did Shakespeare "believe in" the resurrection of the body? We cannot know, but I find nothing in the plays or poems to suggest a consistent supernaturalism in their author, and more perhaps to intimate a pragmatic nihilism. There is no more spiritual comfort to be gained from *Macbeth* than from the other high tragedies. Graham Bradshaw subtly argues that the *terrors* of *Macbeth* are Christian, yet he also endorses Friedrich Nietzsche's reflections on the play in Nietzsche's *Daybreak* (1881). Here is section 240 of *Daybreak:*

> *On the morality of the stage.*—Whoever thinks that Shakespeare's theatre has a moral effect, and that the sight of Macbeth irresistibly repels one from the evil of ambition, is in error: and he is again in error if he thinks Shakespeare himself felt as he feels. He who is really possessed by raging ambition beholds this its image with *joy,* and if the hero perishes by his passion this precisely is the sharpest spice in the hot draught of this joy. Can the poet have felt otherwise? How royally, and not at all like a

rogue, does his ambitious man pursue his course from the moment of his great crime! Only from then on does he exercise "demonic" attraction and excite similar natures to emulation—demonic means here: in defiance *against* life and advantage for the sake of a drive and idea. Do you suppose that Tristan and Isolde are preaching *against* adultery when they both perish by it? This would be to stand the poets on their head: they, and especially Shakespeare, are enamoured of the passions as such and not least of their death-welcoming moods—those moods in which the heart adheres to life no more firmly than does a drop of water to a glass. It is not the guilt and its evil outcome they have at heart, Shakespeare as little as Sophocles (in Ajax, Philoctetes, Oedipus): as easy as it would have been in these instances to make guilt the lever of the drama, just as surely has this been avoided. The tragic poet has just as little desire to take sides *against* life with his images of life! He cries rather: "it is the stimulant of stimulants, this exciting, changing, dangerous, gloomy and often sun-drenched existence! It is an adventure to live—espouse what party in it you will, it will always retain this character!"—He speaks thus out of a restless, vigorous age which is half-drunk and stupefied by its excess of blood and energy—out of a wickeder age than ours is: which is why we need first to *adjust* and *justify* the goal of a Shakespearean drama, that is to say, not to understand it.

Nietzsche links up here with William Blake's adage that the highest art is immoral, and that "Exuberance is beauty." *Macbeth* certainly has "an excess of blood and energy"; its terrors may be more Christian than Greek or Roman, but indeed they are so primordial that they seem to me more shamanistic than Christian, even as the "terms divine" of Sonnet 146 impress me as rather more Platonic than Christian. Of all Shakespeare's plays, *Macbeth* is most "a tragedy of blood," not just in its murders but in the ultimate implications of Macbeth's imagination itself being bloody. The usurper Macbeth moves in a consistent phantasmagoria of blood: blood is the prime constituent of his imagination. He *sees* that what opposes him is blood in one aspect—call it nature in the sense that he opposes nature—and that this opposing force thrusts him into shedding more blood: "It will have blood, they say: blood will have blood."

Macbeth speaks these words in the aftermath of confronting Banquo's ghost, and as always his imaginative coherence overcomes his cognitive confusion. "It" is blood as the natural—call that King Duncan—and the second "blood" is all that Macbeth can experience. His usurpation of Duncan transcends the politics of the kingdom, and threatens a natural good deeply embedded in the Macbeths, but which they have abandoned, and which Macbeth now seeks to destroy, even upon the cosmological level, if only he could. You can call this natural good or first sense of "blood" Christian, if you want to, but Christianity is a revealed religion, and Macbeth rebels against nature *as he imagines it*. That pretty much makes Christianity as irrelevant to *Macbeth* as it is to *King Lear,* and indeed to all the Shakespearean tragedies. Othello, a Christian convert, falls away not from Christianity but from his own better nature, while Hamlet is the apotheosis of all natural gifts, yet cannot abide in them. I am not suggesting here that Shakespeare himself was a gnostic, or a nihilist, or a Nietzschean vitalist three centuries before Nietzsche. But as a dramatist, he is just as much all or any of those as he is a Christian. *Macbeth,* as I have intimated before, is anything but a celebration of Shakespeare's imagination, yet it is also anything but a Christian tragedy. Shakespeare, who understood everything that we comprehend and far more (humankind never will stop catching up to him), long since had exorcised Marlowe, and Christian tragedy (however inverted) with him. Macbeth has nothing in common with Tamburlaine or with Faustus. The nature that Macbeth most strenuously violates is his own, but though he learns this even as he begins the violation, he refuses to follow Lady Macbeth into madness and suicide.

Like *A Midsummer Night's Dream* and *The Tempest, Macbeth* is a visionary drama and, difficult as it is for us to accept that strange genre, a visionary tragedy. Macbeth himself is an involuntary seer, almost an occult medium, dreadfully open to the spirits of the air and of the night. Lady Macbeth, initially more enterprising than her husband, falls into a psychic decline for causes more visionary than not. So much are the Macbeths made for sublimity, figures of fiery eros as they are, that their political and dynastic ambitions seem grotesquely inadequate to their mutual desires. Why do they want the crown? Shakespeare's Richard III, still Marlovian, seeks the sweet fruition of an earthly crown, but the Macbeths are not Machiavellian over-reachers, nor are they sadists or power-obsessed as such. Their mutual lust is also a lust for the throne, a desire that is their Nietzschean revenge against time and time's irrefutable declaration: "It was." Shakespeare did not care to clarify the Macbeths' childlessness. Lady Macbeth speaks of having nursed a child, presumably her own but now dead; we are not told that Macbeth is her second husband, but we may take him to be that. He urges her to bring forth men children only, in admiration of her "manly" resolve, yet pragmatically they seem to expect no heirs of their own union, while he fiercely seeks to murder Fleance, Banquo's son, and does destroy Macduff's children. Freud, shrewder on *Macbeth* than on *Hamlet,* called the curse of childlessness Macbeth's motivation for murder and usurpation. Shakespeare left this matter more uncertain; it is a little difficult to imagine Macbeth as a father when he is, at first, so profoundly dependent on Lady Macbeth. Until she goes mad, she seems as much Macbeth's mother as his wife.

Of all Shakespeare's tragic protagonists, Macbeth is the least free. As Wilbur Sanders implied, Macbeth's actions are a kind of falling forward ("falling in space," Sanders called it). Whether or not Nietzsche (and Freud after him) were right in believing that we are lived, thought, and willed by forces not ourselves, Shakespeare anticipated Nietzsche in this conviction. Sanders acutely follows Nietzsche in giving us a Macbeth who pragmatically lacks any will, in contrast to Lady Macbeth, who is a pure will until she breaks apart. Nietzsche's insight may be the clue to the different ways in which the Macbeths desire the crown: she wills it, he wills nothing, and paradoxically she collapses while he grows ever more frightening, outraging others, himself outraged, as he becomes the nothing he projects. And yet this nothingness remains a negative sublime; its grandeur merits the dignity of tragic perspectives. The enigma of *Macbeth,* as a drama, always will remain its protagonist's hold upon our terrified sympathy. Shakespeare surmised the guilty imaginings we share with Macbeth, who is Mr. Hyde to our Dr. Jekyll. Robert Louis Stevenson's marvelous story emphasizes that Hyde is younger than

Jekyll, only because Jekyll's career is still young in villainy while old in good works. Our uncanny sense that Macbeth somehow is younger in deed than we are is analogous. Virtuous as we may (or may not) be, we fear that Macbeth, our Mr. Hyde, has the power to realize our own potential for active evil. Poor Jekyll eventually turns into Mr. Hyde and cannot get back; Shakespeare's art is to suggest we could have such a fate.

Is Shakespeare himself—on any level—also a Dr. Jekyll in relation to Macbeth's Mr. Hyde? How could he not be, given his success in touching a universal negative sublime through having imagined Macbeth's imaginings? Like Hamlet, with whom he has some curious affinities, Macbeth projects an aura of intimacy: with the audience, with the hapless actors, with his creator. Formalist critics of Shakespeare—old guard and new—insist that no character is larger than the play, since a character is "only" an actor's role. Audiences and readers are not so formalistic: Shylock, Falstaff, Rosalind, Hamlet, Malvolio, Macbeth, Cleopatra (and some others) seem readily transferable to contexts different from their dramas. Sancho Panza, as Franz Kafka demonstrated in the wonderful parable "The Truth About Sancho Panza," can become the creator of Don Quixote. Some new and even more Borgesian Kafka must rise among us to show Antonio as the inventor of Shylock, or Prince Hal as the father of Sir John Falstaff.

To call Macbeth larger than his play in no way deprecates my own favorite among all of Shakespeare's works. The economy of *Macbeth* is ruthless, and scholars who find it truncated, or partly the work of Thomas Middleton, fail to understand Shakespeare's darkest design. What notoriously dominates this play, more than any other in Shakespeare, is time, time that is not the Christian mercy of eternity, but devouring time, death nihilistically regarded as finality. No critic has been able to distinguish between death, time, and nature in *Macbeth;* Shakespeare so fuses them that all of us are well within the mix. We hear voices crying out the formulas of redemption, but never persuasively, compared with Macbeth's soundings of night and the grave. Technically, the men in *Macbeth* are "Christian warriors," as some critics like to emphasize, but their Scottish medieval Catholicism is perfunctory. The kingdom, as in *King Lear,* is a kind of cosmological wasteland, a creation that was also a fall, in the beginning.

Macbeth is very much a night piece; its Scotland is more a mythological Northland than the actual nation from which Shakespeare's royal patron emerged. King James I doubtless prompted some of the play's emphases, but hardly the most decisive, the sense that the night has usurped the day. Murder is the characteristic action of *Macbeth:* not just King Duncan, Banquo, and Lady Macduff and her children are the victims. By firm implication, every person in the play is a potential target for the Macbeths. Shakespeare, who perhaps mocked the stage horrors of other dramatists in his *Titus Andronicus,* experimented far more subtly with the aura of murderousness in *Macbeth.* It is not so much that each of us in the audience is a potential victim. Rather more uneasily, the little Macbeth within each theatergoer can be tempted to surmise a murder or two of her or his own.

I can think of no other literary work with *Macbeth*'s power of *contamination,* unless it be Herman Melville's *Moby-Dick,* the prose epic profoundly influenced by *Macbeth.* Ahab is another visionary maniac, obsessed with what seems a malign order in the universe. Ahab strikes through the mask of natural appearances, as Macbeth does, but the White Whale is no easy victim. Like Macbeth, Ahab is outraged by the equivocation of the fiend that lies like truth, and yet Ahab's prophet, the Parsi harpooner Fedallah himself is far more equivocal than the Weird Sisters. We identify with Captain Ahab less ambivalently than we do with King Macbeth, since Ahab is neither a murderer nor a usurper, and yet pragmatically Ahab is about as destructive as Macbeth: all on the *Pequod,* except for Ishmael the narrator, are destroyed by Ahab's quest. Melville, a shrewd interpreter of Shakespeare, borrows Macbeth's phantasmagoric and proleptic imagination for Ahab, so that both Ahab and Macbeth become world destroyers. The Scottish heath and the Atlantic Ocean amalgamate: each is a context where preternatural forces have outraged a sublime consciousness, who fights back vainly and unluckily, and goes down to a great defeat. Ahab, an American Promethean, is perhaps more hero than villain, unlike Macbeth, who forfeits our admiration though not our entrapped sympathy.

William Hazlitt remarked of Macbeth that "he is sure of nothing but the present moment." As the play progresses to its catastrophe, Macbeth loses even that certitude, and his apocalyptic anxieties prompt Victor Hugo's identification of Macbeth with Nimrod, the Bible's first hunter of men. Macbeth is worthy of the identification: his shocking vitality imbues the violence of evil with biblical force and majesty, giving us the paradox that the play seems Christian not for any benevolent expression but only insofar as its ideas of evil surpass merely naturalistic explanations. If any theology is applicable to *Macbeth,* then it must be the most negative of theologies, one that excludes the incarnation. The cosmos of *Macbeth,* like that of *Moby-Dick,* knows no savior; the heath and the sea alike are great shrouds, whose dead will not be resurrected.

God is exiled from *Macbeth* and *Moby-Dick,* and from *King Lear* also. Exiled, not denied or slain; Macbeth rules in a cosmological emptiness where God is lost, either too far away or too far within to be summoned back. As in *King Lear,* so in *Macbeth:* the moment of creation and the moment of fall fuse into one. Nature and man alike fall into time, even as they are created.

No one desires *Macbeth* to lose its witches, because of their dramatic immediacy, yet the play's cosmological vision renders them a little redundant.

Between what Macbeth imagines and what he does, there is only a temporal gap, in which he himself seems devoid of will. The Weird Sisters, Macbeth's Muses, take the place of that will; we cannot imagine them appearing to Iago, or to Edmund, both geniuses of the will. They are not hollow men; Macbeth is. What happens to Macbeth is inevitable, despite his own culpability, and no other play by Shakespeare, not even the early farces, moves with such speed (as Samuel Coleridge noted). Perhaps the rapidity augments the play's terror; there seems to be no power of the mind over the universe of death, a cosmos all but identical both with Macbeth's phantasmagoria and with the Weird Sisters.

Shakespeare grants little cognitive power to anyone in *Macbeth,* and least of all to the protagonist himself. The intellectual powers of Hamlet, Iago, and Edmund are not relevant to Macbeth and to his play. Shakespeare disperses the energies of the mind, so that no single character in *Macbeth* represents any particular capacity for understanding the tragedy, nor could they do better in concert. Mind is elsewhere in *Macbeth,* it has forsaken humans and witches alike, and lodges freestyle where it will, shifting capriciously and quickly from one corner of the sensible emptiness to another. Coleridge hated the Porter's scene (2.3), with its famous knocking at the gate, but Coleridge made himself deaf to the cognitive urgency of the knocking. Mind knocks, and breaks into the play, with the first and only comedy allowed in this drama. Shakespeare employs his company's leading clown (presumably Robert Armin) to introduce a healing touch of nature where *Macbeth* has intimidated us with the preternatural, and with the Macbeths' mutual phantasmagoria of murder and power:

Porter Here's a knocking indeed! If a man were porter of Hell gate, he should have old turning the key. (*Knocking within*) Knock, knock, knock! Who's there, i' the name of Beelzebub? Here's a farmer, that hanged himself on the expectation of plenty. Come in time. Have napkins enow about you: here you'll sweat for't. (*Knocking within*) Knock, knock! Who's there, in the other devil's name? Faith, here's an equivocator, that could swear in both the scales against either scale, who committed treason enough for God's sake, yet could not equivocate to heaven: O, come in, equivocator. (*Knocking within*) Knock, knock, knock! Who's there? Faith, here's an English tailor come hither, for stealing out of a French hose. Come in, tailor. Here you may roast your goose. (*Knocking within*) Knock, knock; never at quiet! What are you? But this place is too cold for Hell. I'll devil porter it no further: I had thought to have let in some of all professions that go the primrose way to the everlasting bonfire. (*Knocking within*) Anon, anon! I pray you, remember the porter.

[2.3.1–20]

Cheerfully hungover, the Porter admits Macduff and Lennox through what indeed is now Hell gate, the slaughterhouse where Macbeth has murdered the good Duncan. Shakespeare may well be grimacing at himself on "a farmer, that hanged himself on the expectation of plenty," since investing in grain was one of Shake-speare's favorite risks of venture capital. The more profound hu-mor comes in the proleptic contrast between the Porter and Macbeth. As keeper of Hell gate, the Porter boisterously greets "an equivocator," presumably a Jesuit like Father Garnet, who as-serted a right to equivocal answers so as to avoid self-incrimina-tion in the Gunpowder Plot trial of early 1606, the year *Macbeth* was first performed. Historicizing *Macbeth* as a reaction to the Gunpowder Plot to me seems only a compounding of darkness with darkness, since Shakespeare always transcends commentary on his own moment in time. We rather are meant to contrast the hard-drinking Porter with Macbeth himself, who will remind us of the Porter, but not until act 5, scene 5, when Birnam Wood comes to Dunsinane and Macbeth begins: "To doubt the equiv-ocation of the fiend / That lies like truth." Thomas De Quincey confined his analysis of the knocking at the gate in *Macbeth* to the shock of the four knocks themselves, but as an acute rhetori-cian he should have attended more to the Porter's subsequent di-alogue with Macduff, where the Porter sends up forever the no-tion of "equivocation" by expounding how alcohol provokes three things:

Porter Marry, sir, nose painting, sleep, and urine. Lechery, sir, it provokes, and unprovokes. It provokes the desire, but it takes away the performance. Therefore, much drink may be said to be an equivocator with lechery: It makes him, and it mars him; it sets him on, and it takes him off; it persuades him, and disheartens him; makes him stand to, and not stand to; in conclusion, equivocates him in a sleep, and, giving him the lie, leaves him.

[2.3.26–33]

Drunkenness is another equivocation, provoking lust but then denying the male his capacity for performance. Are we perhaps made to wonder whether Macbeth, like Iago, plots murderously because his sexual capacity has been impaired? If you have a proleptic imagination as intense as Macbeth's, then your desire or ambition outruns your will, reaching the other bank, or shoal, of time all too quickly. The fierce sexual passion of the Macbeths possesses a quality of baffled intensity, possibly related to their childlessness, so that the Porter may hint at a situation that transcends his possible knowledge, but not the audience's surmises.

Macbeth's ferocity as a killing machine exceeds even the capacity of such great Shakespearean butchers as Aaron the Moor and Richard III, or the heroic Roman battle prowess of Antony and of Coriolanus. Iago's possible impotence would have some relation to the humiliation of being passed over for Cassio. But if Macbeth's manhood has been thwarted, there is no Othello for him to blame; the sexual victimization, if it exists, is self-generated by an imagination so impatient with time's workings that it always overprepares every event. This may be an element in Lady Macbeth's taunts, almost as if the manliness of Macbeth can be restored only by his murder of the sleeping Duncan, whom Lady Macbeth cannot slay because the good king resembles *her* father in his slumber. The mounting nihilism of Macbeth, which will culminate in his image of life as a tale signifying nothing, perhaps then has more affinity with Iago's devaluation of reality than with Edmund's cold potency.

A. C. Bradley found in *Macbeth* more of a "Sophoclean irony" than anywhere else in Shakespeare, meaning by such irony an augmenting awareness in the audience far exceeding the protagonist's consciousness that perpetually he is saying one thing, and meaning more than he himself understands in what he says. I agree with Bradley that *Macbeth* is the masterpiece of Shakespearean irony, which transcends dramatic, or Sophoclean, irony. Macbeth consistently says more than he knows, but he also imagines more than he says, so that the gap between his overt consciousness and his imaginative powers, wide to begin with, becomes extraordinary. Sexual desire, particularly in males, is likely to manifest all the vicissitudes of the drive when that abyss is so vast. This may be part of the burden of Lady Macbeth's lament before the banquet scene dominated by Banquo's ghost:

> Nought's had, all's spent,
> Where our desire is got without content.
> 'Tis safer to be that which we destroy
> Than by destruction dwell in doubtful joy.
>
> [3.2.4–7]

The madness of Lady Macbeth exceeds a trauma merely of guilt; her husband consistently turns from her (though never against her) once Duncan is slain. Whatever the two had intended by the mutual "greatness" they had promised each other, the subtle irony of Shakespeare reduces such greatness to a pragmatic desexualization once the usurpation of the crown has been realized. There is a fearful pathos in Lady Macbeth's cries of "To bed," in her madness, and a terrifying proleptic irony in her earlier outcry "Unsex me here." It is an understatement to aver that no other author's sense of human sexuality equals Shakespeare's in scope and in precision. The terror that we experience, as audience or as readers, when we suffer *Macbeth* seems to me, in many ways, sexual in its nature, if only because murder increasingly becomes Macbeth's mode of sexual expression. Unable to beget children, Macbeth slaughters them.

Though it is traditional to regard *Macbeth* as being uniquely terri-fying among Shakespeare's plays, it will appear eccentric that I should regard this tragedy's fearsomeness as somehow sexual in its origins and in its dominant aspects. The violence of *Macbeth* doubtless impresses us more than it did the drama's contemporary audiences. Many if not most of those who attended *Macbeth* also joined the large crowds who thronged public executions in Lon-don, including drawings-and-quarterings as well as more civi-lized beheadings. The young Shakespeare, as we saw, probably heaped up outrages in his *Titus Andronicus* both to gratify his au-dience and to mock such gratification. But the barbarities of *Titus Andronicus* are very different in their effect from the savageries of *Macbeth,* which do not move us to nervous laughter:

> For brave Macbeth—well he deserves that name—
> Disdaining Fortune, with his brandished steel,
> Which smoked with bloody execution,
> Like valor's minion carved out his passage
> Till he faced the slave—
> Which ne'er shook hands, nor bade farewell to him,
> Till he unseamed him from the nave to th' chops,
> And fixed his head upon our battlements.
>
> [1.2.16–23]

I cannot recall anyone else in Shakespeare who sustains a death wound from the navel all the way up to his jaw, a mode of un-seaming that introduces us to Macbeth's quite astonishing feroc-ity. "Bellona's bridegroom," Macbeth is thus the husband to the war goddess, and his unseaming strokes enact his husbandly func-tion. Devoted as he and Lady Macbeth palpably are to each other, their love has its problematic elements. Shakespeare's sources gave

him a Lady Macbeth previously married, and presumably griev-
ing for a dead son by that marriage. The mutual passion between
her and Macbeth depends upon their dream of a shared "greatness," the promise of which seems to have been an element in
Macbeth's courtship, since she reminds him of it when he wavers.
Her power over him, with its angry questioning of his manliness,
is engendered by her evident frustration—certainly of ambition,
manifestly of motherhood, possibly also of sexual fulfillment. Victor
Hugo, when he placed Macbeth in the line of Nimrod, the Bible's
first "hunter of men," may have hinted that few of them have been
famous as lovers. Macbeth sees himself always as a soldier, therefore not cruel but professionally murderous, which allows him to
maintain also a curious, personal passivity, almost more the dream
than the dreamer. Famously a paragon of courage and so no coward, Macbeth nevertheless is in a perpetual state of fear. Of what?
Part of the answer seems to be his fear of impotence, a dread related as much to his overwhelming power of imagination as to his
shared dream of greatness with Lady Macbeth.

Critics almost always find an element of sexual violence in
Macbeth's murder of the sleeping and benign Duncan. Macbeth
himself overdetermines this critical discovery when he compares
his movement toward the murder with "Tarquin's ravishing
strides" on that tyrant's way to rape the chaste Lucrece, heroine of
Shakespeare's poem. Is this a rare, self-referential moment on
Shakespeare's own part, since many in Macbeth's audience would
have recognized the dramatist's reference to one of his nondramatic works, which was more celebrated in Shakespeare's time
than it is in ours? If it is, then Shakespeare brings his imagination
very close to Macbeth's in the moment just preceding his protagonist's initial crime. Think how many are murdered onstage in

Shakespeare, and reflect why we are not allowed to watch Macbeth's stabbings of Duncan. The unseen nature of the butchery allows us to imagine, rather horribly, the location and number of Macbeth's thrusts into the sleeping body of the man who is at once his cousin, his guest, his king, and symbolically his benign father. I assumed that, in *Julius Caesar*, Brutus's thrust was at Caesar's privates, enhancing the horror of the tradition that Brutus was Caesar's natural son. The corpse of Duncan is described by Macbeth in accents that remind us of Antony's account of the murdered Caesar, yet there is something more intimate in Macbeth's phrasing:

> Here lay Duncan,
> His silver skin laced with his golden blood,
> And his gashed stabs looked like a breach in nature
> For ruin's wasteful entrance.
>
> [2.3.110–113]

Macbeth and "ruin" are one, and the sexual suggestiveness in "breach in nature" and "wasteful entrance" is very strong, and counterpoints itself against Lady Macbeth's bitter reproaches at Macbeth's refusal to return with the daggers, which would involve his seeing the corpse again. "Infirm of purpose!" she cries out to him first, and when she returns from planting the daggers, her imputation of his sexual failure is more overt: "Your constancy / Hath left you unattended," another reminder that his firmness has abandoned him. But perhaps desire, except to perpetuate himself in time, has departed forever from him. He has doomed himself to be the "poor player," an overanxious actor always missing his cues. Iago and Edmund, in somewhat diverse ways, were both playwrights staging their own works, until Iago was unmasked by Emilia and Edmund received his death wound from the nameless knight, Edgar's disguise. Though Iago and Edmund also played brilliantly in their self-devised roles, they slowed their genius primarily as plotters. Macbeth plots incessantly, but cannot make the drama go as he wishes. He botches it perpetually, and grows more and more outraged that his bloodiest ideas, when accomplished, trail behind them a residuum that threatens him still. Malcolm and Donalbain, Fleance and Macduff—all flee, and their survival is for Macbeth the stuff of nightmare.

Nightmare seeks Macbeth out; that search, more than his violence, is the true plot of this most terrifying of Shakespeare's plays. From my childhood on, I have been puzzled by the Witches, who spur the rapt Macbeth on to his sublime but guilty project. They come to him because preternaturally they *know* him: he is not so much theirs as they are his. This is not to deny their reality apart from him, but only to indicate again that he has more implicit power over them than they manifest in regard to him. They place nothing in his mind that is not already there. And yet they undoubtedly influence his total yielding to his own ambitious imagination. Perhaps, indeed, they are the final impetus that renders Macbeth so ambiguously passive when he confronts the phantasmagorias that Lady Macbeth says always have attended him. In that sense, the Weird Sisters are close to the three Norns, or Fates, that William Blake interpreted them as being: they gaze into the seeds of time, but they also act upon those they teach to gaze with them. Together with Lady Macbeth, they persuade Macbeth to his self-abandonment, or rather they prepare Macbeth for Lady Macbeth's greater temptation into unsanctified violence.

Surely the play inherits their cosmos, and not a Christian universe. Hecate, goddess of spells, is the deity of the night world, and though she calls Macbeth "a wayward son," his actions pragmatically make him a loyal associate of the evil sorceress. One senses, in rereading *Macbeth,* a greater preternatural energy within Macbeth himself than is available to Hecat or to the Weird Sisters. Our equivocal but compulsive sympathy for him is partly founded upon Shakespeare's exclusion of any other human center of interest, except for his prematurely eclipsed wife, and partly upon our fear that his imagination is our own. Yet the largest element in our irrational sympathy ensues from Macbeth's sublimity. Great utterance continuously breaks through his confusions, and a force neither divine nor wicked seems to choose him as the trumpet of its prophecy:

> Besides, this Duncan
> Hath borne his faculties so meek, hath been
> So clear in his great office, that his virtues
> Will plead like angels, trumpet tongued, against
> The deep damnation of his taking off,
> And pity, like a naked newborn babe
> Striding the blast, or heaven's cherubim, horsed
> Upon the sightless couriers of the air,
> Shall blow the horrid deed in every eye,
> That tears shall drown the wind.

> [1.7.16–25]

Here, as elsewhere, we do not feel that Macbeth's proleptic eloquence is inappropriate to him; his language and his imaginings are those of a seer, which heightens the horror of his disintegration into the bloodiest of all Shakespearean tyrant-villains. Yet we wonder just how and why this great voice breaks through Macbeth's consciousness, since clearly it comes to him unbidden.

He is, we know, given to seizures; Lady Macbeth remarks, "My Lord is often thus, / And hath been from his youth." Visionary fits come upon him when and as *they* will, and his tendency to second sight is clearly allied both to his proleptic imaginings and to the witches' preoccupation with him. No one else in Shakespeare is so occult, not even the hermetic magician, Prospero.

This produces an extraordinary effect upon us, since we *are* Macbeth, though we are pragmatically neither murderers nor mediums, and he is. Nor are we conduits for transcendent energies, for visions and voices; Macbeth is as much a natural poet as he is a natural killer. He cannot reason and compare, because images beyond reason and beyond competition overwhelm him. Shakespeare can be said to have conferred his own intellect upon Hamlet, his own capacity for more life upon Falstaff, his own wit upon Rosalind. To Macbeth, Shakespeare evidently gave over what might be called the passive element in his own imagination. We cannot judge that the author of *Macbeth* was victimized by his own imagination, but we hardly can avoid seeing Macbeth himself as the victim of a beyond that surmounts anything available to us. His tragic dignity depends upon his contagious sense of unknown modes of being, his awareness of powers that lie beyond Hecat and the witches but are not identical with the Christian God and his angels. These powers are the tragic sublime itself, and Macbeth, despite his own will, is so deeply at one with them that he can contaminate us with sublimity, even as the unknown forces contaminate him. Critics have never agreed as to how to name those forces; it seems to me best to agree with Nietzsche that the prejudices of morality are irrelevant to such daemons. If they terrify us by taking over this play, they also bring us joy, the utmost pleasure that accepts contamination by the daemonic.

Macbeth, partly because of this uncanniness, is fully the rival of *Hamlet* and of *King Lear,* and like them transcends what might seem the limits of art. Yet the play defies critical description and analysis in ways very different from those of *Hamlet* and *Lear.* Hamlet's inwardness is an abyss; Lear's sufferings finally seem more than human; Macbeth is all too human. Despite Macbeth's violence, he is much closer to us than are Hamlet and Lear. What makes this usurper so intimate for us? Even great actors do badly in the role, with only a few exceptions, Ian McKellen being much the best I've attended. Yet even McKellen seemed haunted by the precariousness of the role's openness to its audience. I think we most identify with Macbeth because we also have the sense that we are violating our own natures, as he does his. *Macbeth,* in another of Shakespeare's startling originalities, is the first expressionist drama. The consciousness of Hamlet is wider than ours, but Macbeth's is not; it seems indeed to have exactly our contours, whoever we are. And as I have emphasized already, the proleptic element in Macbeth's imagination reaches out to our own apprehensiveness, our universal sense that the dreadful is about to happen, and that we have no choice but to participate in it.

When Malcolm, at the play's end, refers to "this dead butcher and his fiend-like queen," we are in the odd position both of having to agree with Duncan's son and of murmuring to ourselves that so to categorize Macbeth and Lady Macbeth seems scarcely adequate. Clearly the ironies of *Macbeth* are not born of clashing perspectives but of divisions in the self—in Macbeth and in the audience. When Macbeth says that in him "function is smothered in surmise," we have to agree, and then we brood on to what more limited extent this is true of ourselves also. Dr. Johnson said that in *Macbeth* "the events are too great to admit the influence of particular dispositions." Since no one feared more than Johnson what he called "the dangerous prevalence of the imagination," I have to assume that the greatest of all critics wished not to acknowledge that the particular disposition of Macbeth's proleptic imagination overdetermines the events of the play. Charting some of the utterances of this leaping-ahead in Macbeth's mind ought to help us to leap ahead in his wake.

In a rapt aside, quite early in the play, Macbeth introduces us to the extraordinary nature of his imagination:

> This supernatural soliciting
> Cannot be ill, cannot be good. If ill,
> Why hath it given me earnest of success,
> Commencing in a truth? I am Thane of Cawdor.
> If good, why do I yield to that suggestion
> Whose horrid image doth unfix my hair,
> And make my seated heart knock at my ribs,
> Against the use of nature? Present fears
> Are less than horrible imaginings.
> My thought, whose murder yet is but fantastical,
> Shakes so my single state of man that function
> Is smother'd in surmise, and nothing is
> But what is not.
>
> [1.3.130–142]

"My single state of man" plays upon several meanings of "single": unitary, isolated, vulnerable. The phantasmagoria of murdering Duncan is so vivid that "nothing is / But what is not," and "function," the mind, is smothered by "surmise," fantasy. The dramatic music of this passage, impossible not to discern with the inner ear, is very difficult to describe. Macbeth speaks to himself in a kind of trance, halfway between trauma and second sight. An involuntary visionary of horror, he *sees* what certainly is going to happen, while still knowing this murder to be "but fantastical." His tribute to his own "horrible imaginings" is absolute: the implication is that his will is irrelevant. That he stands on the border of madness may seem evident to us now, but such a judgment would be mistaken. It is the resolute Lady Macbeth who goes mad; the proleptic Macbeth will become more and more outraged and outrageous, but he is no more insane at the close than he is here. The parameters of the diseased mind waver throughout Shakespeare. Is Hamlet ever truly mad, even north-by-northwest? Lear, Othello, Leontes, Timon all pass into derangement and (partly) out again, but Lady Macbeth is granted no recovery. It might be a relief for us if Macbeth ever went mad, but he cannot, if only because he represents all our imaginations, including our capacity for anticipating futures we both wish for and fear.

At his castle, with Duncan as his royal guest, Macbeth attempts a soliloquy in Hamlet's mode, but rapidly leaps into his own:

> If it were done when 'tis done, then 'twere well
> It were done quickly. If th' assassination
> Could trammel up the consequence, and catch
> With his surcease success, that but this blow
> Might be the be-all and the end-all—here,
> But here, upon this bank and shoal of time,
> We'd jump the life to come.
>
> [1.7.1–7]

"Jump" partly means "risk," but Shakespeare carries it over into our meaning also. After the great vision of "pity, like a naked newborn babe" descends upon Macbeth from some transcendent realm, the usurping host has another fantasy concerning his own will:

> I have no spur
> To prick the sides of my intent, but only
> Vaulting ambition, which o'erleaps itself
> And falls on the other—
>
> [1.7.25–28]

Lady Macbeth then enters, and so Macbeth does not complete his metaphor. "The other" what? Not "side," for his horse, which is all will, has had its sides spurred, so that ambition evidently is now on the other shoal or shore, its murder of Duncan established as a desire. That image is central in the play, and Shakespeare takes care to keep it phantasmagoric by not allowing us to see the actual murder of Duncan. On his way to this regicide, Macbeth has a vision that takes him even further into the realm where "nothing is, but what is not":

> Is this a dagger which I see before me,
> The handle toward my hand? Come, let me clutch thee.
> I have thee not, and yet I see thee still.
> Art thou not, fatal vision, sensible
> To feeling as to sight? Or art thou but
> A dagger of the mind, a false creation,
> Proceeding from the heat oppressèd brain?
> I see thee yet, in form as palpable
> As this which now I draw.
> Thou marshall'st me the way that I was going,
> And such an instrument I was to use.
> Mine eyes are made the fools o' the other senses,
> Or else worth all the rest. I see thee still,
> And on thy blade and dudgeon gouts of blood,
> Which was not so before. There's no such thing.
> It is the bloody business which informs

Thus to mine eyes. Now o'er the one halfworld
Nature seems dead, and wicked dreams abuse
The curtained sleep. Witchcraft celebrates
Pale Hecat's offerings, and withered murder,
Alarumed by his sentinel, the wolf,
Whose howl's his watch, thus with his stealthy pace,
With Tarquin's ravishing strides, towards his design
Moves like a ghost. Thou sure and firm set earth,
Hear not my steps, which way they walk, for fear
Thy very stones prate of my whereabout,
And take the present horror from the time,
Which now suits with it. Whiles I threat, he lives:
Words to the heat of deeds too cold breath gives.

A BELL RINGS

I go, and it is done. The bell invites me.
Hear it not, Duncan, for it is a knell
That summons thee to heaven, or to hell.

[2.1.32–63]

This magnificent soliloquy, culminating in the tolling of the bell, always has been judged to be an apotheosis of Shakespeare's art. So accustomed is Macbeth to second sight that he evidences neither surprise nor fear at the visionary knife but coolly attempts to grasp this "dagger of the mind." The phrase "a false creation" subtly hints at the gnostic cosmos of *Macbeth,* which is the work of some demiurge, whose botchings made creation itself a fall. With a wonderful metaphysical courage, admiration for which helps implicate us in Macbeth's guilts, he responds to the phantasmagoria by drawing his own dagger, thus acknowledging his oneness with his own proleptic yearnings. As in *King Lear,* the primary meaning of *fool* in this play is "victim," but Macbeth defiantly asserts the possibility that his eyes, rather than being victims, may be worth all his other senses together.

This moment of bravura is dispersed by a new phenomenon in Macbeth's visionary history, as the hallucination undergoes a temporal transformation, great drops of blood manifesting themselves upon blade and handle. "There's no such thing," he attempts to insist, but yields instead to one of those openings-out of eloquence that perpetually descend upon him. In that yielding to Hecat's sorcery, Macbeth astonishingly identifies his steps toward the sleeping Duncan with Tarquin's "ravishing strides" toward his victim in Shakespeare's narrative poem *The Rape of Lucrece*. Macbeth is not going to ravish Duncan, except of his life, but the allusion would have thrilled many in the audience. I again take it that this audacity is Shakespeare's own signature, establishing his complicity with his protagonist's imagination. "I go, and it is done" constitutes the climactic prolepsis; we participate, feeling that Duncan is dead already, before the thrusts have been performed.

It is after the next murder, Banquo's, and after Macbeth's confrontation with Banquo's Ghost, that the proleptic utterances begin to yield to the usurper's sense of being more outraged than outrageous:

> Blood hath been shed ere now, i' the olden time,
> Ere humane statute purged the gentle weal.
> Ay, and since too, murders have been performed
> Too terrible for the ear. The time has been
> That, when the brains were out, the man would die,
> And there an end, but now they rise again,
> With twenty mortal murders on their crowns,

And push us from our stools. This is more strange
Than such a murder is.

[3.4.78–86]

Since moral contexts, as Nietzsche advised us, are simply irrelevant to *Macbeth,* its protagonist's increasing sense of outrage is
perhaps not as outrageous as it should be. The witches equivocate
with him, but they are rather equivocal entities in any case; I like
Bradshaw's remark that they "seem curiously capricious and in-
fantile, hardly less concerned with pilots and chestnuts than with
Macbeth and Scotland." Far from governing the *kenoma,* or cosmological emptiness, in which *Macbeth* is set, they seem much
punier components of it than Macbeth himself. A world that fell
even as it was created is anything but a Christian nature. Though
Hecat has some potency in this nature, one feels a greater demi-
urgical force at loose in this play. Shakespeare will not name it, except to call it "time," but that is a highly metaphorical time, not
the "olden time" or good old days, when you bashed someone's
brains out and so ended them, but "now," when their ghosts dis-
place us.

That "now" is the empty world of *Macbeth,* into which we, as
audience, *have been thrown,* and that sense of "thrownness" *is* the
terror that Wilbur Sanders and Graham Bradshaw emphasize in
Macbeth. When Macduff has fled to England, Macbeth chills us
with a vow: "From this moment / The very firstlings of my heart
shall be / The firstlings of my hand." Since those firstlings pledge
the massacre of Lady Macduff, her children, and all "unfortunate
souls" related to Macduff, we are to appreciate that the heart of
Macbeth is very much also the heart of the play's world. Macbeth's beheading by Macduff prompts the revenger, at the end, to
proclaim, "The time is free," but we do not believe Macduff. How

can we? The world is Macbeth's, precisely as he imagined it; only the kingdom belongs to Malcolm. *King Lear,* also set in the cosmological emptiness, is too various to be typified by any single utterance, even of Lear's own, but Macbeth concentrates his play and his world in its most famous speech:

> She should have died hereafter.
> There would have been a time for such a word.
> Tomorrow, and tomorrow, and tomorrow
> Creeps in this petty pace from day to day,
> To the last syllable of recorded time,
> And all our yesterdays have lighted fools
> The way to dusty death. Out, out, brief candle.
> Life's but a walking shadow, a poor player
> That struts and frets his hour upon the stage
> And then is heard no more. It is a tale
> Told by an idiot, full of sound and fury,
> Signifying nothing.
>
> [5.5.17–28]

Dr. Johnson, rightly shocked that this should be Macbeth's response to the death of his wife, at first insisted that "such a word" was an error for "such a world." When the Grand Cham retreated from this emendation, he stubbornly argued that "word" meant "intelligence" in the sense of "information," and so did not refer to "hereafter," as, alas, it certainly does. Johnson's moral genius was affronted, as it was by the end of *King Lear,* and Johnson was right: neither play sees with Christian optics. Macbeth has the authority to speak for his play and his world, as for his self. In Macbeth's time there is no hereafter, in any world. And yet this is the suicide of his own wife that has been just reported to him. Grief, in any sense we could apprehend, is not expressed by him. Instead of an elegy for Queen Macbeth, we hear a nihilistic death march, or rather a creeping of fools, of universal victims. The "brief candle" is both the sun and the individual life, no longer the "great bond" of Macbeth's magnificent invocation just before Banquo's murder:

> Come, seeling night,
> Scarf up the tender eye of pitiful day,
> And with thy bloody and invisible hand
> Cancel and tear to pieces that great bond
> Which keeps me pale! Light thickens, and the crow
> Makes wing to th' rooky wood.
> Good things of day begin to droop and drowse,
> Whiles night's black agents to their preys do rouse.
> Thou marvell'st at my words. But hold thee still.
> Things bad begun make strong themselves by ill.
>
> [3.2.46–55]

There the night becomes a royal falcon rending the sun apart, and Macbeth's imagination is wholly apocalyptic. In the "Tomorrow, and tomorrow, and tomorrow" chant, the tenor is postapocalyptic, as it will be in Macbeth's reception of the news that Birnam Wood has come to Dunsinane: "I gin to be aweary of the sun, / And wish the estate o' the world were now undone."

Life is a walking shadow in that sun, a staged representation like the bad actor whose hour of strutting and fretting will not survive our leaving the theater. Having carried the reverberation of Ralph Richardson as Falstaff in my ear for half a century, I reflect (as Shakespeare, not Macbeth, meant me to reflect) that Richardson will not be "heard no more" until I am dead. Macbeth's finest verbal coup is to revise his metaphor; life suddenly is no longer a bad actor, but an idiot's story, nihilistic of necessity.

The magnificent language of Macbeth and of his play is reduced to "sound and fury," but that phrase plays back against Macbeth, his very diction, in all its splendor, refuting him. It is as though he at last refuses himself any imaginative sympathy, a refusal impossible for his audience to make.

I come back, for a last time, to the terrible awe that Macbeth provokes in us. G. Wilson Knight first juxtaposed a reflection by Lafew, the wise old nobleman of *All's Well That Ends Well,* with *Macbeth:*

Lafew They say miracles are past; and we have our philosophical
    persons to make modern and familiar, things supernatural and
    causeless. Hence is it that we make trifles of terrors,
    ensconcing ourselves into seeming knowledge, when we
    should submit ourselves to an unknown fear.

                                     [2.3.1–6]

Wilbur Sanders, acknowledging Wilson Knight, explores *Macbeth* as the Shakespearean play where most we "submit ourselves to an unknown fear." My own experience of the play is that we rightly react to it with terror, even as we respond to *Hamlet* with wonder. Whatever *Macbeth* does otherwise, it certainly does not offer us a catharsis for the terrors it evokes. Since we are compelled to internalize Macbeth, the "unknown fear" finally is of ourselves. If we submit to it—and Shakespeare gives us little choice—then we follow Macbeth into a nihilism very different from the abyss-voyages of Iago and of Edmund. They are confident nihilists, secure in their self-election. Macbeth is never secure, nor are we, his unwilling cohorts; he childers, as we father, and we are the only children he has.

The most surprising observation on fear in *Macbeth* was also

Wilson Knight's: "Whilst Macbeth lives in conflict with himself there is misery, evil, fear; when, at the end, he and others have openly identified himself with evil, he faces the world fearless: nor does he appear evil any longer."

I think I see where Wilson Knight was aiming, but a few revisions are necessary. Macbeth's broad progress is from proleptic horror to a sense of baffled expectations, in which a feeling of having been outraged takes the place of fear. "Evil" we can set aside; it is redundant, rather like calling Hitler or Stalin evil. When Macbeth is betrayed, by hallucination and foretelling, he manifests a profound and energetic outrage, like a frantic actor always fated to miss all his cues. The usurper goes on murdering, and achieves no victory over time or the self. Sometimes I wonder whether Shakespeare somehow had gotten access to the gnostic and manichaean fragments scattered throughout the church fathers, quoted by them only to be denounced, though I rather doubt that Shakespeare favored much ecclesiastical reading. Macbeth, however intensely we identify with him, is more frightening than anything he confronts, thus intimating that we ourselves may be more dreadful than anything in our own worlds. And yet Macbeth's realm, like ours, can be a ghastly context:

Old Man Threescore and ten I can remember well,
  Within the volume of which time I have seen
  Hours dreadful and things strange. But this sore night
  Hath trifled former knowings.
Ross   Ah, good father,
  Thou seest the heavens, as troubled with man's act,
  Threaten his bloody stage. By the clock, 'tis day,
  And yet dark night strangles the traveling lamp.

Is't night's predominance, or the day's shame,
That darkness does the face of earth entomb,
When living light should kiss it?
Old Man   'Tis unnatural,
Even like the deed that's done. On Tuesday last,
A falcon, towering in her pride of place,
Was by a mousing owl hawked at and killed.
Ross   And Duncan's horses—a thing most strange and
certain—
Beauteous and swift, the minions of their race,
Turned wild in nature, broke their stalls, flung out,
Contending 'gainst obedience, as they would make
War with mankind.
Old Man   'Tis said they eat each other.
Ross   They did so, to the amazement of mine eyes
That look'd upon 't.

[2.4.1–20]

This is the aftermath of Duncan's murder, yet even at the play's opening a wounded captain admiringly says of Macbeth and Banquo: "they doubly redoubled strokes upon the foe. / Except they meant to bathe in reeking wounds, / Or memorize another Golgotha, / I cannot tell." What does it mean to "memorize another Golgotha"? Golgotha, "the place of skulls," was Calvary, where Jesus suffered upon the cross. "Memorize" here seems to mean "memorialize," and Shakespeare subtly has invoked a shocking parallel. We are at the beginning of the play, and these are still the *good* captains Macbeth and Banquo, patriotically fighting for Duncan and for Scotland, yet they are creating a new slaughter ground for a new crucifixion. Graham Bradshaw aptly has described the horror of nature in *Macbeth,* and Robert Watson has pointed to its gnostic affinities. Shakespeare throws us into everything that is not ourselves, not so as to induce an ascetic revulsion in the audience, but so as to compel a choice between Macbeth and the cosmological emptiness, the *kenoma* of the gnostics. We choose Macbeth perforce, and the preference is made very costly for us.

Of the aesthetic greatness of *Macbeth,* there can be no question. The play cannot challenge the scope and depth of *Hamlet* and *King Lear,* or the brilliant painfulness of *Othello,* or the world-without-end panorama of *Antony and Cleopatra,* and yet it is my personal favorite of all the high tragedies. Shakespeare's final strength is radical internalization, and this is his most internalized drama, played out in the guilty imagination that we share with Macbeth. No critical method that works equally well for Thomas Middleton or John Fletcher and for Shakespeare is going to illuminate Shakespeare for us. I do not know whether God created Shakespeare, but I know that Shakespeare created us, to an altogether startling degree. In relation to us, his perpetual audience, Shakespeare is a kind of mortal god; our instruments for measuring him break when we seek to apply them. *Macbeth,* as its best critics have seen, scarcely shows us that crimes against nature are repaired when a legitimate social order is restored. Nature *is* crime in *Macbeth,* but hardly in the Christian sense that calls out for nature to be redeemed by grace, or by expiation and forgiveness. As in *King Lear,* we have no place to go in *Macbeth;* there is no sanctuary available to us. Macbeth himself exceeds us, in energy and in torment, but he also represents us, and we discover him more vividly within us the more deeply we delve.

FURTHER READING

Basic

Furness, Horace Howard, ed. *"Macbeth": The New Variorum Edition.*
New York: Dover, 1963.

Hinman, Charlton. *The First Folio of Shakespeare.* 2d ed. Introduction by
Peter W. M. Blayney. New York: W. W. Norton, 1996.

Onions, C. T. *A Shakespeare Glossary.* Enlarged and revised by Robert D.
Eagelson. Oxford: Clarendon Press, 1986.

Oxford English Dictionary on CD-Rom, version 3.0. 2d ed. New York:
Oxford University Press, 2002.

History and Commentary

Barroll, Leeds. *Politics, Plague, and Shakespeare's Theater: The Stuart Years.*
Ithaca, N.Y.: Cornell University Press, 1991.

Berryman, John. *Berryman's Shakespeare.* Edited by John Haffenden,
Preface by Robert Giroux. New York: Farrar, Straus and Giroux,
1999.

Chandos, John, ed. *In God's Name: Examples of Preaching in England,
1534–1662.* Indianapolis, Ind.: Bobbs-Merrill, 1971.

Cohn, Norman. *Europe's Inner Demons: An Enquiry Inspired by the Great
Witch-Hunt.* New York: Basic, 1975.

Coulton, G. G. *Five Centuries of Religion.* 4 vols. Vol. 1. Cambridge:
Cambridge University Press, 1923.

Cressy, David. Birth, *Marriage and Death: Ritual, Religion, and the Life-Cycle in Tudor and Stuart England.* Oxford: Oxford University Press, 1997.

Ellis, Alexander J. *On Early English Pronunciation, with Especial Reference to Shakspere and Chaucer.* Part One. London: Trübner, 1867.

Ellis, Henry, ed. *Original Letters, Illustrative of English History.* 3d ser. Vol. 4. London: Richard Bentley, 1846.

Flint, Valerie I. J. *The Rise of Magic in Early Medieval Europe.* Princeton, N.J.: Princeton University Press, 1991.

Goddard, Harold C. *The Meaning of Shakespeare.* 2 vols. Chicago: University of Chicago Press, 1951.

Gurr, Andrew. *Playgoing in Shakespeare's London.* Cambridge: Cambridge University Press, 1987.

———. *The Shakespearian Stage, 1574–1642.* 3d ed. Cambridge: Cambridge University Press, 1992.

Hibbard, G. R. *The Making of Shakespeare's Dramatic Poetry.* Toronto: University of Toronto Press, 1981.

Higham, Florence. *Lancelot Andrewes.* London: SCM Press, 1952.

Kermode, Frank. *Shakespeare's Language.* New York: Farrar, Straus and Giroux, 2000.

Kernan, Alvin. *Shakespeare, the King's Playwright: Theater in the Stuart Court, 1603–1613.* New Haven and London: Yale University Press, 1995.

Knight, G. Wilson. *The Wheel of Fire: Interpretations of Shakespearean Tragedy.* 5th rev. ed. Introduction by T. S. Eliot. New York: Meridian, 1957.

Lanham, Richard A. *The Motives of Eloquence: Literary Rhetoric in the Renaissance.* New Haven and London: Yale University Press, 1976.

McDonald, Russ. *The Bedford Companion to Shakespeare: An Introduction with Documents.* Boston: St. Martin's Press, 1996.

The Malleus Maleficarum of Heinrich Kramer and James Sprenger. Edited and translated by Montague Summers. New York: Dover, 1971.

Rabb, Theodore K. *The Struggle for Stability in Early Modern Europe.* New York: Oxford University Press, 1975.

Raffel, Burton. *From Stress to Stress: An Autobiography of English Prosody.* Hamden, Conn.: Archon, 1992.

————. 1995. "Metrical Dramaturgy in Shakespeare's Earlier Plays." *CEA Critic* 57, no. 3: 51–65.

————. 1996. "Who Heard the Rhymes, and How: Shakespeare's Dramaturgical Signals." *Oral Tradition* 11, no. 2: 190–221.

Siegel, Paul N., ed. *His Infinite Variety: Major Shakespearian Criticism Since Johnson.* Philadelphia: Lippincott, 1964.

Thomas, Keith. *Religion and the Decline of Magic: Studies in Popular Beliefs in Sixteenth and Seventeenth Century England.* New York: Oxford University Press, 1997.

Thomson, Peter. *Shakespeare's Professional Career.* Cambridge: Cambridge University Press, 1992.

Van Doren, Mark. *Shakespeare.* New York: Holt, 1939.

Wells, Stanley, ed. *The Cambridge Companion to Shakespeare Studies.* Cambridge: Cambridge University Press, 1986.

Willbern, David. *Poetic Will: Shakespeare and the Play of Language.* Philadelphia: University of Pennsylvania Press, 1997.

Willey, Basil. *The Seventeenth Century Background: Studies in the Thought of the Age in Relation to Poetry and Religion.* New York: Columbia University Press, 1933.

Wills, Garry. *Witches and Jesuits: Shakespeare's "Macbeth."* New York: Oxford University Press, 1995.

Woodbridge, Linda. *The Scythe of Saturn: Shakespeare and Magical Thinking.* Urbana: University of Illinois Press, 1994.

FINDING LIST

Repeated unfamiliar words and their meanings, alphabetically arranged, by act, scene, and footnote number of first occurrence, in the spelling (and grammatical form) of that first occurrence

all hail	1.3.51	*cousin*	1.2.3
anon	1.1.9	*crown*	1.5.44
art	1.2.14	*doubt* (verb)	4.2.31
attend	1.5.17	*drowsy*	3.2.43
battlements	1.2.35	*earnest* (noun)	1.3.96
become	1.2.63	*ere*	1.1.4
before	1.4.20	*esteem* (verb)	1.7.53
betimes	3.4.124	*fair*	1.1.10
bid (verb)	1.6.24	*fatal*	1.5.41
business	1.5.79	*fantastical*	1.3.5
but (only)	2.1.45	*feast* (noun)	2.2.45
charged	5.1.17	*file* (noun)	3.1.108
clear	1.5.83	*free*	2.1.17
confusion	2.3.68	*gashes*	1.2.62
contend	1.3.85	*gentle*	2.3.83
corporal	1.3.75	*gentleman*	1.2.38

harbinger	1.4.60	purposes (verb)	1.5.70
hie (verb)	1.5.25	rapt	1.3.60
heath	1.1.6	shall	1.3.79
issue	3,1,66	slave	1.2.29
kerns	1.2.19	sooth	1.2.5
kites	3.4.74	sprites	2.3.79
knell	2.1.86	stand	3.3.5
mark	1.2.43	state	1.4.35
methought	2.2.39	station (noun)	3.1.118
ministers	1.5.56	stay (verb)	1.3.14
morrow	1.5.72	stick (verb)	3.1.48
mortal (adjective)	3,4,79	straight (adverb)	3.1.157
nothing (adverb)	1.3.90	time (noun)	1.5.75
office	1.7.26	timely	4.3.61
once	4.3.148	unnatural	2.4.13
owed (verb)	1.4.12	wants (verb)	3.4.135
pains	1.3.106	way	1.3.72
partner	1.3.57	weal	3.4.76
peace	1.3.40	wherefore	2.2.34
perfect	3.1.127	withal	2.1.13
present	1.2.9	within	1.2.3
prithee	1.7.58	(stage direction)	
protest (verb)	3.4.95	without	3.1.43
purged	3.4.76	worthy	1.2.38
purpose (noun)	1.5.51	wrack	1.3.103